HAYDEN ENGLISH LANGUAGE SERIES

Robert W. Boynton — Consulting Editor

Former Principal, Senior High School
and Chairman, English Department
Germantown Friends School

AN INTRODUCTION TO MODERN ENGLISH GRAMMAR
J. Malmstrom

LANGUAGE IN SOCIETY (Rev. 2nd Ed.)
J. Malmstrom

WORDS, WORDS, WORDS:
Vocabularies and Dictionaries (Rev. 2nd Ed.)
R. Lodwig and E. Barrett

WRITING TO BE READ
K. Macrorie

TELLING WRITING
K. Macrorie

ENGLISH I and II: A Contemporary Approach
R. W. Boynton, R. Johnson, and R. Reeves

WORKOUTS IN READING AND WRITING
O. B. Davis

COMPOSING: Writing as a Self-Creating Process
W. E. Coles, Jr.

COMPOSING:
Writing as a Self-Creating Process

William E. Coles, Jr.
Professor of English, Director of Composition
University of Pittsburgh

HAYDEN BOOK COMPANY, INC.
Rochelle Park, New Jersey

For Theodore Baird

Library of Congress Cataloging in Publication Data

Coles, William E
  Composing: writing as a self-creating process.

  (Hayden English language series)
  Teacher's ed. issued under title: Teaching composing.
  1. English language—Rhetoric. 2. College readers.
I. Title
[PE1417.C636]   808′ .04275   74-10987
ISBN 0-8104-5838-1

    1 2 3 4 5 6 7 8 9 PRINTING

   74 75 76 77 78 79 80 81 82 YEAR

Acknowledgments

For Assignment 28, for the idea for the assignments on rote learning, and for the passages quoted in Assignments 6 and 18, I am indebted to Professor Theodore Baird of Amherst College.

For the diagram of the Perfect Student, and for the idea for Assignments 1 and 7, I am indebted to Professor John F. Butler of George Peabody College for Teachers.

Contents

To the Student   1

1 Teaching and Learning: Expectations   6

2 Holding Hands   7

3 Really Knowing   9

4 A Change of Mind 11

5 Rote Learning 13

6 Rote Learning and History 14

7 The Telephone Dial 15

8 Rote Learning and Writing 18

9 Children's Writing 20

10 The Theme: What Is It? 23

11 Malcolm X 27

12 Benjamin Franklin (Part I) 30

13 Benjamin Franklin (Part II) 35

14 D. H. Lawrence 37

15 The Perfect Student 40

16 S. H. Hadley 42

17 A Madman 45

18 A Good Teacher 47

19 Wilder and Agassiz 50

20 Shaler and Agassiz 51

21 Teaching and Learning: A Situation 55

22 A Flash of Insight 57

23 Writing as Learning 58

24 Why Doesn't Education Work Better? 63

25 Lewis Padgett 64

26 Edward Gorey 94

27 Seeing Other Ways of Seeing 112

28 The Man from Mars 114

29 The Risk of Education 116

30 Putting Things Together 119

To the Student

The assignments of this text are designed to be used for a course in writing, a course in which writing, specifically your writing, is the center. Their aim is to offer you an opportunity to become a better reader and writer, first by giving you a meaningful subject to read and write about, and second, by making it possible for you to use your attempts to improve yourself as a reader and a writer to learn something about language and yourself as a language user: what language is, how it functions, why it is important. In practice you will find that these two aims become reflexes of each other. To become more knowledgeable about language is to increase your ability to manipulate it, just as to become a better reader and writer is to enlarge your understanding of the nature of language and its significance in your life. One learns to read and write by reading and writing—and by taking seriously, because he understands the importance of taking seriously, what it is he is doing.

The nominal subject of the assignments is teaching and learning. This subject provides you with something relevant to your immediate experience to think and write about, and serves also to give class conversation a focus, the day by day movement of a course some kind of shape and direction. But the real subject of the assignments is language, and their real function is to involve you with the activity of language using, of *composing* in the largest sense of the word. They are constructed to give you the chance to work out in your own terms and for yourself what it means to see yourself as a composer of your own reality. For composed this reality is, composed by language, or more accurately by languages, those various arrangements of terminologies or names or symbols (whatever you may wish to call them) with which each one of us frames and organizes the world he lives in and by which, for better or for worse, each one of us is framed and organized.

The idea behind this way of seeing writing is that you will have a better chance to write better sentences if you have some idea of what a sentence is, and of what it can mean to write one, than if you don't. For simply to write sentences, all of them for someone else, with no consciousness of what the activity can involve or of how it can be important, is as meaningless as it is boring; and it is hard to imagine how anyone for whom the activity of writing is no more than this could care very much about writing at all, let alone whether he gets any better at it. But to understand the activity of writing in such a way as to develop a consciousness of oneself as a manipulator of language and of his experience as arranged, defined, and evaluated by the languages which shape it, is to have the chance to discover also the ways in which one's identity as a person is dependent upon the languages he commands. This consciousness, which the assignments are contrived in a variety of ways to move you toward, will not automatically make you a writer, but it can provide you with the chance to understand the activity of writing as an activity with meaning—as important for what it is *about* as for what it is. It can provide you with the chance to understand, in whatever language you work with, at least the significance of creating a voice of your own.

These assignments, then, are intended for a course in writing that is a course in language as well: a course in composing, selecting and arranging, putting together. The medium of communication you will be working with is largely the English language—largely though not entirely, for in addressing some assignments you may wish to use colored pencils and crayons to make sketches; or perhaps you may choose to express relationships in mathematical notation or with equations. And even though it is with experience expressed in terms of words, sentences, paragraphs, with the workings of the English langauge, that most of the assignments concern themselves, these operations are looked at in such a way as to invite you to understand them as common to the workings of language in general—whether that language is made up of mathematical or chemical symbols, shapes and colors on canvas, gestures, or words. The assignments, in other words, seek to make it possible for a future physicist, say, through his attempts to improve himself in English, to become more responsible to himself as a user of the language of physics.

The emphasis here, you will notice, falls heavily on the notion of invitation, on the assignments as offering you a chance or an opportunity. This is deliberate and is intended as a compliment. In certain courses, and at certain levels of education, the substance of knowledge—what the participants in the process are to think about—is supplied by the teacher or the textbook; the term paper, the quiz, and the examination then serve to measure how much has been retained by the student of what has been transmitted to him. But with these assignments nothing is transmitted to you, nothing is demanded of you in this way. In order to deal with them you will be supplying your own information and material. After all, you have held various jobs and played games. You live in a variety of communities. And for a number of years now you have had your own thoughts and feelings about things. This is your experience, and from this seemingly shapeless and yet entirely individual source you will derive whatever it is you have to say. In this sense, all of the questions of all of the assignments may be understood to involve the same issues: where and how with this problem do you locate your self? To what extent and in what ways is this self definable in language? What is this self on the basis of the language shaping it here? What has it got to do with you?

You should understand that the self being spoken of above, and the one that you will be concerned with in the classroom, is a literary self; not a mock or false self, but a stylistic self, the self construable from the way words fall in a conversation or on a page. The other self, your identity as a person, is something that no teacher as a teacher can have very much to do with. That there is a relation between these two selves, between writing and thinking, intellect and being, a very complicated and involving relation indeed—this is undeniable. This relation, in fact, is the center of both the assignments as assignments and the assignments as more than that. But the nature of this relation, that of the self to the roles or styles in which it finds expression and through which it grows, is one that only an individual writer or thinker has the right to work out, and it can hardly become the province of public discourse without a teacher's ceasing to be a teacher, a student's ceasing to be a student. Ideally, hopefully, primarily, the concern of the assignments is with words; not with thinking, but with a language about thinking; not with people or selves, but with languages about people and selves. If your teacher seems to refuse, therefore, either to sympathize with or to condemn a self outside the words it has chosen to have shape, it is because he believes that you are a person as well as a student, that you have a life as well as roles, and a life that no one has the right to interfere with. Few teachers are either equipped for or ready to assume the responsibility of posing as parents, priests, or psychoanalysts.

While you supply the material for your own discourse, the assignments are contrived both to direct a general movement from day to day throughout the term and to enable you to move from their nominal subject to their real one. In this sense the assignments have a chronology. They are arranged. The first few assignments, for example, ask you to isolate a bit of your experience and then ask you something about what you have done in this act of separating one thing from another, of arranging what you know in some sort of pattern. Subsequent assignments provide you with additional perspectives from which to question this pattern, to widen or narrow or otherwise revise it if you want to. How you put together the materials given you to work with in an assignment, what you choose to deal with and what you choose to ignore in the questions asked of you, what form you will give to the papers you write—these are matters that most of the time will be left strictly up to you. That is, the problems you will be addressing will be up to you in a certain sense to formulate. As you move from assignment to assignment you will be making increasingly complicated statements about yourself as a writer, a composer, a language user—statements which you will be asked finally to take into consideration in making some sort of order out of your experience with the assignments as a whole, some sort of sense of where you started with them and of where you seem to come out.

It must be emphatically said that the assignments themselves are not an argument. They contain no doctrine, either individually or as a sequence. There is no philosophy in them, either homespun or highflown, for a teacher to become aware of and give to students, for students to become aware of and give back to a teacher. Above all, the questions of the assignments must be understood as invariably open, as questions to be addressed rather than answered. In fact, the assignments are arranged and phrased precisely to make impossible the discovery in them of anything like a master plan. They are put together in such a way as to mean only and no more than what the various responses they are constructed to evoke can be made to mean, a meaning that will be different for different teachers and students as well as differently come by. In a paper addressed, for example, to Assignment 15, a student may work out a connection with a paper that he (or someone else) wrote for Assignment 7, which at Assignment 20, after a discussion of Assignment 19, may be the subject of a paper in which he changes his interpretation of the problem of Assignment 5. Other students may move in other ways.

Thus, at the same time that the creation of some pattern for your experience with the assignments will be necessary if you are to make anything of them at all, an infinite number of patterns for them is possible. This is not to say, of course, that every pattern, every way of addressing a question, is as good as every other, but it is to say that whatever continuity you construct from assignment to assignment, from one paper to another, from one class discussion to the next, is your continuity and yours alone. It is this continuity, this meaning, which in expressing your understanding of yourself as a language user will express also what you make your experience with the subject of composing mean to you. Whatever you learn from your experience with these assignments, you learn. Whatever you make of your awareness of the activity of writing as an activity of language is up to you.

Since the assignments exist to make possible a number of different ways of talking about what they are about, there is no one way to use them, nothing in them that cannot be rearranged, rephrased, added to, or deleted as the style of a teacher, the length of a term, the requirements of a course, or the character of a class determines. Your teacher may have you focus on a single aspect of an assignment, for example, rather than work with it as a totality. Or you may be asked to work with passages other than or in addition to those provided by the text. Perhaps your teacher will alter the order of the assignments or construct some of his own to replace or supplement what is here. And because each assignment is designed to be used as either a writing assignment or a class exercise, something to talk through in discussion, it will have to be decided how many papers you are going to write and which assignments you will address these papers to. This text, in other words, is not itself a composition course. It merely provides the materials for one.

Your teacher will read your papers, comment on them, and bring examples of your writing to class to talk about. In your attempts to improve yourself as a writer, to enlarge your understanding of the nature and function of language in your life, he will be of what help to you he can. But do not expect him to tell you how to proceed with an assignment, how to find something in your experience to talk about, or how to make a given issue relevant or meaningful in terms of your own life. No one can do this for another. For the same reason it is unreal to expect that your teacher will be able to tell you how to improve your writing. If anyone could tell someone else how to do this, then courses in writing would not be necessary. The best a teacher can do, a course can do, an education can do, is to put you in a position to improve yourself for yourself—and be ready to acknowledge your effort.

1. Teaching and Learning: Expectations

In order to write papers for a course in writing, you must make a start somewhere. Our subject is language, but the metaphor we will be using in order to try to understand a little of how we use words, how we define words and make sense, is the process of teaching and learning. The assignments, then, are a means of starting a conversation about our subject, starting it and keeping it going. If you consider each paper you write as something less than a final pronouncement, less the means of closing a question than of keeping it open, you will put yourself in a position to learn more.

*   *   *

This writing assignment is for the purpose of sorting you out as individuals. Your paper will be read as soon as you have written it, but will not be returned to you until later in the term.

(Have your English teachers in the past always returned your work to you right away? Do you find yourself at all suspicious of the claim that "your paper will be read as soon as you have written it"?)

Although most of your experience with formal education has been required of you by law, you are now at the stage of having a choice of whether to continue with it or not. This means that you have certainly speculated, however remotely, on why you are now attending an educational institution instead of doing something else, on what it is you imagine you are doing here, on the meaning of a formal education in the context of your own life.

Address yourself to what you expect of the process of teaching and learning in the time you will spend here. What is it you want to learn exactly? How do you propose to go about doing it? Do you intend to do as you're told, is that what learning consists of? Or do you intend to do something other than what you're told? Is there anything you would like to learn in your formal education that you doubt you can? And what do you expect of your teachers? Are they to provide information only? Are they to interfere with your way of thinking? Do you have an idea of what a Good Teacher is? What's a Good Student?

If you find it difficult to draw lines here, face your puzzlement squarely. What is it that you find baffling or perplexing about such a subject? It is, after all, your education you're talking about.

2. Holding Hands

Before a large public audience, a Famous Man recently started a speech by saying:

> Holding hands is not really so easy a thing to do as many people think. How to hold hands is something a person must learn.

This statement was greeted with long applause by all elements of the audience. Without knowing more than what you are told here about those elements, speculate on why the speaker was applauded. To do this, consider the following information and questions.

1. In the audience was a group of young people, aged 17 to 21 (mostly college students), many of whom would be called "hippies" by older people. A number of these people applauded vigorously, some of them looking with scorn at the over-40 members of the audience. What do you suppose these applauding young people took the speaker's statement to mean?

2. Why do you suppose that a number of them looked with scorn at the over-40s?

3. Many of the over-40s also applauded. The speaker himself was over 50. What do you suppose these applauding over-40s took the speaker to mean?

4. Some of the applauding over-40s sneered back at the young people, as if in triumph. What do you suppose they thought their triumph consisted of?

5. Also in the audience was a small group of people who were in the middle of a week-long Sensitivity Training Workshop. They *stood* and applauded, but instead of sneering at others, they looked as if they felt pity for them. What do you suppose this group took the speaker to mean?

6. Why do you suppose they looked with pity on the others?

7. To judge from the speaker's sentences quoted at the beginning of this exercise, can *you* tell what he means?

8. Do you see any way that the people in the audience could tell what the speaker meant any better than you can?

9. Then how do you account for such different groups of people with such (presumably) different sets of values behaving as they did?

10. Now, back to our story. Upon hearing the applause of the audience, the Famous Man quoted above stopped, smiled, and then simply sat down. At that point, all elements of the audience applauded even more enthusiastically. What do you suppose the various elements of the audience took the speaker's smiling and sitting down to mean?

11. What do you think the speaker's smiling and sitting down might have meant?

12. The speaker used language, or more accurately languages. To interpret him, the audience also used language. From this point of view, what does the phenomenon you have been considering here enable you to conclude about the nature and function of language?

13. Can you conclude anything about the importance of language to teaching? To learning?

3. Really Knowing

Here is what a teacher of writing has to say of the papers he wrote as a student for an English course in college:

> . . . My own papers in that course were generally regurgitated liberalism. . . . There was nothing in them that came from my own experience, my own notions of what would constitute evidence for my conclusions. There I was, in Utah in the depths of the depression, writing about the Okies when I could have been writing about the impoverished farmers all around me. I wrote about race relations in the South without ever having talked with a Negro in my life and without recognizing that the bootblack I occasionally saw in Salt Lake City in the Hotel Utah was in any way related to the problem of race relations. . . . My life, my observations, my insights were not included in those papers on the Okies and race relations and the New Deal. Every opinion was derivative, every observation second-hand. . . . What I wrote was therefore characterless, without true personality, though often full of personal pronouns.
>
> —*Wayne Booth* *

An obvious conclusion to be drawn from Booth's evaluation of his work is that he was not writing about his own experience, about what he really knew of the world around him. (And why not, do you imagine? Did he have a Bad English Teacher? A Poor Background? Was he just Lazy? Any other possibilities?) It is no surprise, therefore, to find him advising teachers of writing to get their students "to write about something they know about."

Papers about ideas written by sheep are boring; papers written by thinking boys and girls are interesting. The problem is always to find ideas at a level that will allow the student to reason, that is, to provide support for his ideas, rather than merely assert them in half-baked form. And this means something that is all too often forgotten by the most ambitious teachers—namely, that whatever ideas the student writes about must somehow be connected with his own experience.*

---

* Excerpts from "Boring from Within: The Art of the Freshman Essay," by Wayne C. Booth are reprinted from *The Norton Reader,* third edition, Arthur M. Eastman, Gen. Ed. By permission of W. W. Norton & Company, Inc. Copyright © 1973, 1969, 1965 by W. W. Norton & Company, Inc.

If you were to apply these remarks to your own activity as a writer, what would you say you really "know about"? What "ideas" would you point to as being "connected with [your] own experience"? How would you talk about them?

Choose such an idea, something you feel you really "know about," and write a paper in which you make clear exactly how the idea is connected with your life as you are living it.

On the basis of what you have written, can you see any reason for your having pointed where you have?

4. A Change of Mind

A common way of speaking of a moment of learning something is to say, "I changed my mind." Let it be granted that we do not say this about all acts of learning, but about some we certainly do. Here is a section of a poem which can be read as a description of such a moment.

> One summer evening (led by her°) I found
> A little boat tied to a willow tree
> Within a rocky cove, its usual home.
> Straight I unloosed her chain, and stepping in
> Pushed from the shore. It was an act of stealth
> And troubled pleasure, nor without the voice
> Of mountain-echoes did my boat move on;
> Leaving behind her still, on either side,
> Small circles glittering idly in the moon,
> Until they melted all into one track
> Of sparkling light. But now, like one who rows,
> Proud of his skill, to reach a chosen point
> With an unswerving line, I fixed my view
> Upon the summit of a craggy ridge,
> The horizon's utmost boundary; far above
> Was nothing but the stars and the grey sky.
> She was an elfin pinnace; lustily
> I dipped my oars into the silent lake,
> And, as I rose upon the stroke, my boat
> Went heaving through the water like a swan;
> When, from behind that craggy steep till then
> The horizon's bound, a huge peak, black and huge,
> As if with voluntary power instinct,
> Upreared its head. I struck and struck again,
> And growing still in stature the grim shape
> Towered up between me and the stars, and still,
> For so it seemed, with purpose of its own
> And measured motion like a living thing,
> Strode after me. With trembling oars I turned,
> And through the silent water stole my way
> Back to the covert of the willow tree;
> There in her mooring-place I left my bark,—
> And through the meadows homeward went, in grave

° Nature.

And serious mood; but after I had seen
That spectacle, for many days, my brain
Worked with a dim and undetermined sense
Of unknown modes of being; o'er my thoughts
There hung a darkness, call it solitude
Or blank desertion. No familiar shapes
Remained, no pleasant images of trees,
Of sea or sky, no colours of green fields;
But huge and mighty forms, that do not live
Like living men, moved slowly through the mind
By day, and were a trouble to my dreams.

—*William Wordsworth* *

From the speaker's point of view, and right from the start ("It was an act of stealth/And troubled pleasure"), his taking the boat for a row on the lake seems to have felt like a kind of stealing. He takes the boat anyway, but then after rowing for a while apparently changes his mind about what he is doing and returns it. The following questions are for the purpose of helping you determine what seems to be involved in Wordsworth's creation of this experience seen as a change of mind.

After taking the boat, how does the speaker seem at first to feel about what he is doing? How does he describe his surroundings, for example? What seems to be his attitude toward the boat, the act of rowing?

How does the speaker name his surroundings finally? What state of mind does his new terminology for his surroundings seem to suggest he is in?

What is it exactly that decides the speaker to return the boat, that seems to change his mind about what he is doing? There is that "huge peak," but is it possible for a detail of landscape to bring about a change of mind?

*   *   *

Write an account as if it were a scene in a short story of a moment in your experience when you learned something and said (or now feel you could have said), "I changed my mind." Give all the relevant particulars. Tell where you were, what was going on, what you were doing, who else was there, what happened, how you changed your mind.

To judge from what you have written, what exactly was involved in this learning experience? There was a change. You saw things one way and then you saw things another way. But what exactly was this mind you changed? From what to what did you change it?

What do you now say that the phrase "to change your mind" means?

* From William Wordsworth, *The Prelude,* Book One, lines 357–400.

5. Rote Learning

Go back to the remarks of Wayne Booth quoted in Assignment 3. Consider the kind of learning he says he poured into those papers on the Okies and race relations: "Every opinion was derivative; every observation second-hand." This is usually known as rote-learned knowledge or as rote learning.

Consider your attitudes toward rote learning. How much of your past education would you say has consisted of it? (This question asks for a quantitative answer and you can only make an estimate.) How are you accustomed to hearing it talked about? Are you used to hearing it praised by your teachers, by your family, by your fellow students? Or is it something you expect to hear condemned? How do you feel about it yourself?

6. Rote Learning and History

Here is an anecdote about Charles Edward Garman as a student in the Yale Divinity School. (The date is about 1872.)

> Early in the session . . . Professor Fisher asked us to read fifty pages in his book, *The Beginnings of Christianity,* and the next day called on Garman to recite first. Garman began with the first line and went through to the end of the hour *verbatim et literatim.**

This is told in admiration, as evidence of a fine mind, a remarkable intelligence. Plainly, at one time in the educational system the exact use of the memory was highly valued. It is not so long ago, not much more than forty years, that Yale University operated on the systems of "recitations." Although reciting what has been learned in the textbook has not been much used in colleges and schools for some time, it was probably the rule for most of the 19th century and for many centuries before that. Interestingly, when Garman became a professor himself, he did not use the recitation method.

Suppose that in one of your classes someone began to recite page after page of the "outside readings." There would be no question here of cheating. How would such a frank display of the memory be greeted by teacher and students? How would you respond to it?

What do you suppose has happened in the world? Why is the recitation no longer the normal way of conducting a class? Look at this problem historically: What has happened since 1872 or thereabouts?

* From *Letters, Lectures, and Addresses of Charles Edward Garman,* Boston, 1909, p. 13.

7. The Telephone Dial (Part I)

We turn now to an example of your own rote learning. Do you remember how old you were when you first learned to use the telephone? And you have been using it ever since, for fifteen years, more or less, how many times a month, a week, a day?

The circular dialing mechanism of the telephone is an apparatus with which you have had a great deal of experience. You can close your eyes and visualize it, can you not? Half asleep you could call Seattle. Or Bangkok. Perhaps you are so familiar with the telephone that you could dial a number in the dark if you had to. Why, a mere child . . .

Take ten minutes or so right now in order to sketch from memory the standardized circular dialing mechanism that you use so often and know so well. Include all the numbers and letters as you remember them. The right-angled coordinates below are for the purpose of enabling you to make your circles as true as possible. Scale your model in any way that you wish, but try to keep the various parts of your model as proportionate to one another as you can. When you've gone as far with your sketch as you think you can go, turn to Part II of this assignment.

7. The Telephone Dial (Part II)

Check the sketch you made of the dialing mechanism of the telephone against the real thing. Did you make any mistakes? Of what sort? (The usual number of errors, by the way, is about two dozen.) Did you know that there was no dialing hole at twelve o'clock? Did you remember that the letters Q and Z are not used in the system? How about the relationship of the numbers to the letters, did you get that right? Does your sketch indicate that the lettering order reverses itself at M? The little white (or black) dot at the center of the dialing holes: Was that in your drawing? Did you know that that dot cost the telephone company upward of a quarter of a million dollars in research money to place where it is, and that it is said to save the company millions of dollars a year in preventing misplaced telephone calls? Could your sketch of the telephone dial serve as the model for a telephone? Could you call Seattle on such a telephone?

If you made mistakes in your sketch, how do you account for the fact that you made the mistakes you did? Can you see any pattern in them? Do you think that after checking your sketch against the dial that you could make a more accurate model than you first did. Why? Are there some mistakes you are convinced you wouldn't, won't, make a second time? Why?

There are certain details of the telephone dial that you got right in your sketch, that almost anybody would. Which ones? How do you account for the fact that you got them right, for your certainty that almost anyone would?

Perhaps there are certain details you got right that you are not convinced everybody would. If so, if you knew for certain what letters weren't used in the dialing system, for example, how did you know it? What makes you uncertain whether others would know what you know?

You will notice that this assignment is worded in such a way as to allow for the possibility of someone's having made an accurate sketch of the telephone dial. Speculate for a moment on who such a person might be? Are such terms as Genius, Photographic Memory, Mental Picture, and the like of much help to you with such a question?

You have rote-learned how to use the telephone dialing mechanism. (Is it something you really know?) You know what the telephone dial looks like. But what is it that you rote-learned? What is it that you show in your sketch you knew, exactly?

Look back at the papers you have written for this course so far. To judge from what you have written, have you rote-learned anything else in the way that you rote-learned the telephone dial? What does your way of addressing this question enable you to conclude about your relationship to your learning?

8. Rote Learning and Writing

To return to the notion that there are some things you really know, what about writing? Can a knowledge of writing be part of a writer? Can a knowledge of writing be rote-learned? What does it mean to say that it can or cannot?

Let's look at some examples of writing as a way of trying to address these questions. Again, our approach will be historical. We will confine ourselves to the writing of students, all of whom wrote what they did in circumstances much like those in which you find yourself as a student in this course. They were writing required papers for a course in composition.

Here, for instance, is a section of a student's paper submitted in a writing course at Harvard in 1893:

The Paradise of Books

Books, I often think, are the best thing life has to offer us. No where else do we get pleasure that is so great and so lasting, that can charm us still, whatever our condition of mind and body. There we meet friends and lovers such as reality cannot acquaint us with, and adventures which furnish excitement without toil, and arouse sympathy without suffering. All the higher emotions, so incongruous with matter-of-fact existence, may be serenely enjoyed in the realm of poetry, and all the speculative flights which transcend cold common-sense may soar undisturbed in the aether of philosophy. As long as a man has eyes to read and brain to understand, he may feel sure of one unfailing resource which can amply compensate the strokes of fortune.

Here is a section of a paper written by a student in the early 1960s:

What is the alternative to the conflict between nation and nation, Black and White, Gentile and Jew, Parent and Child? It is to put the flower in the gun, to grow a little more sensitive to the needs of others, a little less selfish in the attempt to communicate. It is to recognize that materialism breeds only materialism, and hatred hatred. It is to see as Jesus and Mohammed saw that the needs of mankind can be met . . .

Later in the same decade a student wrote:

Too much violence, eh? What we don't have is enough. Look at King. Look at the Kennedys. Where are they now? Look at what happened to the "Niggers" in Detroit. Look at where wanting the vote got the people of Mississippi. We'll "overcome" when we start to understand that violence is the only thing the People of the United States will listen to. It's the poor and the hungry, those who are jammed into ghettoes by acts of corruption and inequalities of . . .

And not so long ago, a student wrote this:

I believe that the past is tremendously important to the success or failure of everyone later on in his life. My past has taught me many valuable lessons which I will not easily forget. The most important lesson I have learned to date would be with regards to patience. As a boxer will tell you, you have to learn to roll with every punch your opponent throws at you. It is the same in day to day life situations. You should be aware of all around you and keep a relatively rational mind so you can make the right decisions.

How would you characterize the voice you hear speaking in each of the passages above? How do you respond to those voices in each instance? What would you say that the ideal audience for the voice in each case would be? Do you find yourself a member of any of these audiences ever?

The examples given you span almost a century. There are obvious differences between them. But it is also possible to draw some connecting lines here, to see those pieces of writing in similar terms. What terms do you use to connect them? What lines do you draw?

How do you think the writers of each of the passages learned to write as they did? Who do you think taught them, and how was this teaching done? And how about the learning, how was that done?

9. Children's Writing

It has been said that the difference between a child's and an adult's writing is not that one is good and the other bad, for they both may be bad. But a child's writing sometimes shows "a clarity of vision, [a] force of expression, [and] . . . an innocence of imagination that adults might envy." It is also declared that most "children find it hard to go on writing interestingly. . . . Of a sudden, the child is a child no longer" (Boris Ford *).

Boris Ford, you will note, is not a sentimentalist. Children's writing can be bad:

Christmas Eve

It was Christmas Eve.
When you looked out the window
   you could see the lights.
When you looked all around it was
   a beautiful sight.
You could hear bells ringing,
   You could hear people singing.
The snow was so white
   Everything was so bright,
      It was a beautiful sight!

—Dana, age 10

But look at this writing done by children. Both Kathy and Michael are average students—so far as such a term ever meant anything.

If I Were the Snow

If I were the snow
I would snow every
single Christmas.
I would snow on my
brother and make his
toes so red he
would hit me.
I would snow all over the
universe, on Mars,

---

* Boris Ford, *Young Writers, Young Readers*, London, 1960, p. 97. Reprinted by permission of Humanities Press, Inc., New York.

the earth. I would
snow so hard on
the moon, I
would show the man
on there who's boss.
I would not be just white
I'd be red, blue, and
green. I'd be yellow
dots, orange dots
black ones too.
                    —Kathy, age 10 †

Sums

One and Two were playing about in a sum-book. Suddenly
One said, 'I'm older than you because I am fifty, you are only ten!'
Of course Two was very angry. 'I've had enough of you!'
'But that was only in the game,' protested One.
'Game or no game, I've had enough of you. You can go out of
here at once!'
'Boo-Hoo! Don't want to go out of here; want to stay here;
boo-hoo!'
'Well, you're going out of here!' And Two pushed One out and
slammed the door behind him, and locked it firmly!
That evening Twenty came home from work, tired and angry.
'Where is One?' he shouted. (One always pulled up Twenty's chair.)
'Well, father . . .' began Two, when Twenty interrupted: 'No
"wells," where is he?'
'Well, father,' began Two again. 'Well, father, we had a quar-
rel, and I pushed One out!'
'What? Well bring him in!'
So Two went out, and half an hour later came back with One.
'Here he is father,' said Two.
'Good,' thundered father.
Some days later, One and Two were playing. 'I'm older than
you,' said One.
'O.K., have it your own way!' said Two.

                                        —Michael, age 9 ‡

† From *Wishes, Lies and Dreams,* by Kenneth Koch and the Students of P.S. 61
in New York City. Copyright © 1970 by Kenneth Koch. Reprinted by permission of Random House, Inc.

‡ In Boris Ford, *Young Writers, Young Readers, op. cit.,* p. 8.

What do you make of these two pieces? Though you are not accustomed, perhaps, to seeing your study of calculus or physics, say, in relation to your home life or your social situation; though you may not ordinarily think of snow in terms of Mars or colored polka dots—these pieces aren't exactly silly, are they? Do you see anything in them, anything specific, that you might want to call "a clarity of vision" or a "force of expression" or an "innocence of imagination?" Is there anything here you "envy"?

Ford uses the term "child" to make a distinction between ways of seeing and experiencing the world. There is the "child" and then there is "the child [who] is a child no longer." On the basis of your experience with these three pieces of children's writing, explain your understanding of this distinction.

10. The Theme: What Is It?

You know what a sonnet is. Perhaps you can define the terms *short story, novel, play, epic.* Maybe you even know how to describe the heroic couplet as used by Alexander Pope or blank verse by Shakespeare. In other words, you do know something about Literary Forms.

Consider the Literary Form known as *The English Paper* or *Theme.* No one leaves high school without knowing about Themewriting or without knowing how to write a Theme. Indeed, the technique can sometimes be learned a great deal earlier, as early as the age of ten.

Themewriting is a language, a way of experiencing the world. It is nonwriting rather than writing.

Invented originally by English teachers for use in English classrooms only, it is as closed a language as the Dewey Decimal System, as calculatedly dissociated from the concerns of its user and the world he lives in as it has been possible to make it. But the selling points of it as a commodity are irresistible. For since the skill of Themewriting is based upon the use of language conceived of entirely in terms of communication, the only standard that need be applied to it is whether it succeeds in creating in the reader—that is, in another Themewriter—the desired response. The writer's character, personality, moral nature, convictions . . . it is taken for granted are in no way engaged in forming sentences out of words and paragraphs out of sentences. Language is a tool, it is said. Or just a tool. If the reader buys the product or the idea, believes something, feels certain emotions, votes a particular ticket, etc., then the writing is good. Then the English is good.

The selling points of this commodity are not only irresistible, they are undeniable; and so is the utility of what is being sold. Writing seen as a trick that can be played, a device that can be put into operation, is also a technique that can be taught and learned— just as one can be taught or can learn to run an adding machine, or pour concrete. And once equipped with this skill a writer can write a Theme about anything, and at a moment's notice. It is a valuable technique to know, therefore, because like the American dollar it is negotiable anywhere—and its buying power is unlimited. A student can use the technique of Themewriting not only to write papers but to plan a career or a marriage, to organize a life even. And if the standards of this imitation writing are those to which the dignity of full commitment is unthinkable; if the orders won by it are more sterile than the chaos from which they are won; if the price paid to teach this kind of writing, and to learn it, may be more than the chance to be Lively or Interesting; there are few to say so. For to make Themewriting or non-writing stand for writing . . . is to make impossible also the conception of, let alone the demand for, writing as writing inside its circle.

$\qquad$ —*William E. Coles, Jr.**

With Themewriting it is possible not only "to organize a life" for one's self, it is possible also to organize—that does seem the right word —a life for others. Consider the following remarks by George Orwell (from an essay originally published in 1946):

In our time it is broadly true that political writing is bad writing. Where it is not true, it will generally be found that the writer is some kind of rebel, expressing his private opinions and not a "party line." Orthodoxy, of whatever color, seems to demand a lifeless, imitative style. The political dialects to be found in pamphlets, leading articles, manifestos, White Papers and the speeches of under-secretaries do, of course, vary from party to party, but they are all alike in that one almost never finds in them a fresh, vivid, homemade turn of speech. When one watches some tired hack on the platform mechanically repeating the familiar phrases—*bestial atrocities, iron heel, bloodstained tyranny, free peoples of the world, stand shoulder to shoulder*—one often has a curious feeling that one is not watching a live human being but some kind of dummy: a feeling which suddenly becomes stronger at moments when the light catches the speaker's spectacles and turns them into blank discs which seem to have no eyes behind them. And this is not altogether fanciful. A speaker who uses that kind of phraseology has gone some distance towards turning himself into a machine. The appropriate noises are coming out of his larynx, but his brain is not involved as it would be if he were choosing his words for himself. If the speech he is making is one that he is accustomed to make over and over again, he may be almost unconscious of what he is saying, as one is when one utters the responses in church. And this reduced state of consciousness, if not indispensable, is at any rate favorable to political conformity.

In our time, political speech and writing are largely the defence of the indefensible. Things like the continuance of British rule in India, the Russian purges and deportations, the dropping of the atom bombs on Japan, can indeed be defended, but only by arguments

* William E. Coles, Jr., "Freshman Composition: The Circle of Unbelief," *College English*, November, 1969, pp. 136–137. Reprinted with permission of the National Council of Teachers of English.

which are too brutal for most people to face, and which do not square with the professed aims of political parties. Thus political language has to consist largely of euphemism, question-begging and sheer cloudy vagueness. Defenceless villagers are bombarded from the air, the inhabitants driven out into the countryside, the cattle machine-gunned, the huts set on fire with incendiary bullets: this is called *pacification*. Millions of peasants are robbed of their farms and sent trudging along the roads with no more than they can carry: this is called *transfer of population* or *rectification of frontiers*. People are imprisoned for years without trial, or shot in the back of the neck or sent to die of scurvy in Arctic lumber camps: this is called *elimination of unreliable elements*. Such phraseology is needed if one wants to name things without calling up mental pictures of them. . . .

The great enemy of clear language is insincerity. When there is a gap between one's real and one's declared aims, one turns as it were instinctively to long words and exhausted idioms, like a cuttlefish squirting out ink. In our age there is no such thing as "keeping out of politics." All issues are political issues, and politics itself is a mass of lies, evasions, folly, hatred and schizophrenia. When the general atmosphere is bad, language must suffer. I should expect to find—this is a guess which I have not sufficient knowledge to verify—that the German, Russian and Italian languages have all deteriorated in the last ten or fifteen years, as a result of dictatorship.

—George Orwell †

*   *   *

In the technique of Themewriting you need no further training. We are entirely satisfied that you can write a Theme on any given subject. This paper will give you an opportunity to demonstrate your skill with the technique of Themewriting, to share some of your trade secrets. It will give you also an opportunity to come to terms with what it means to have such trade secrets to share.

First of all, play the game for a paragraph. Choose what might seem to be three or four disparate words or terms, terms, that is, with no obvious relationship between them, and list them at the head of your paper. Then make a relationship between the terms in the form of a Lead Sentence that will enable you to write a Theme. Come up with a paragraph that will enable a reader to say: "Yes, it looks like English. It looks like a Theme or the start of one written for an English course."

† Excerpted from "Politics and the English Language" in *Shooting an Elephant and Other Essays* by George Orwell, copyright 1945, 1946, 1949, 1950 by Sonia Brownell Orwell. Reprinted by permission of Harcourt Brace Jovanovich, Inc.

Now, consider how you performed this trick, for trick it is. How did you begin? How did you know how to proceed? What state of mind do you assume to write a Theme? What criticisms do you attempt to forestall? What standards do you try to preserve? For whom are you writing? What good is it?

When you have made up your mind about these matters, express your understanding of what you have done in the form of a diagram or drawing. Or, perhaps, you could develop a mathematical or chemical equation. You may use explanatory words or sentences, but express yourself primarily in a language other than English. Use color if you wish.

Finally, write a paragraph in which you attempt to establish your relationship, not to your example of Themewriting, but to your own writing. What is the nature of this relationship as you see it now? Do you wish that it were other than it is? Why? This is a paragraph in which you can look back over what you have been doing so far this term and draw some conclusions.

11. Malcolm X

Here is a description of a learning experience taken from *The Autobiography of Malcolm X*.*

The experience spoken of took place toward the beginning of Malcolm X's serving a ten year prison term. He had had only an eighth grade education. In his attempts to write letters about "how the white man's society was responsible for the black man's condition in this wilderness of North America" (he wrote to the Mayor of Boston, the Governor of Massachusetts, and the President of the United States among others), he found himself, as he says, "increasingly frustrated at not being able to express what [he] wanted to convey. . . . In the street," he writes, "I had been the most articulate hustler out there—I had commanded attention when I said something. But now, trying to write simple English, I not only wasn't articulate, I wasn't even functional. How would I sound writing in slang, the way I would *say* it, something such as, 'Look, daddy, let me pull your coat about a cat. . . .' " Also, Malcolm X speaks of his "envy" of a fellow prisoner whose "stock of knowledge" enabled him to "take charge of any conversation he was in." In an attempt "to emulate" this prisoner (these are his words "envy" and "emulate"), Malcolm X tried to read what he could, but in skipping the words he didn't understand, he went through, as he puts it, "only book reading motions" and ended up with "little idea" of the meaning of what he had read. In order "to study, to learn some words" (and also "to improve penmanship"), he requested a dictionary along with some tablets and pencils from the prison school. The following is his account of what happened once these materials had been given to him.

I spent two days just riffling uncertainly through the dictionary's pages. I'd never realized so many words existed! I didn't know *which* words I needed to learn. Finally, just to start some kind of action, I began copying.

In my slow, painstaking, ragged handwriting, I copied into my tablet everything printed on that first page, down to the punctuation marks.

I believe it took me a day. Then, aloud, I read back, to myself, everything I'd written on the tablet. Over and over, aloud, to myself, I read my own handwriting.

* From *The Autobiography of Malcolm X* by Malcolm X with the assistance of Alex Haley. Copyright © 1964 by Alex Haley and Malcolm X; copyright © 1965 by Alex Haley and Betty Shabazz. Reprinted by permission of Grove Press, Inc.

I woke up the next morning, thinking about those words—immensely proud to realize that not only had I written so much at one time, but I'd written words I never knew were in the world. Moreover, with a little effort, I also could remember what many of these words meant. I reviewed the words whose meanings I didn't remember. Funny thing, from the dictionary first page right now, that "aardvark" springs to my mind. The dictionary had a picture of it, a long-tailed, long-eared, burrowing African mammal, which lives off termites caught by sticking out its tongue as an anteater does for ants.

I was so fascinated that I went on—I copied the dictionary's next page. And the same experience came when I studied that. With every succeeding page, I also learned of people and places and events from history. Actually the dictionary is like a miniature encyclopedia. Finally the dictionary's A section had filled a whole tablet—and I went on into the B's. That was the way I started copying what eventually became the entire dictionary. It went a lot faster after so much practice helped me to pick up handwriting speed. Between what I wrote in my tablet, and writing letters, during the rest of my time in prison I would guess I wrote a million words.

Throughout his *Autobiography,* Malcolm X speaks of this experience in tones of unmistakable gratitude. He read books too, of course, and talked with many of his fellow prisoners. He debated and took advantage of classes provided by the prison administration. But the act of copying out the dictionary *verbatim* he specifies as a seminal experience in his education.

*   *   *

Do you believe that Malcolm X did what he says he did? In prison one is likely to have time on his hands to be sure, but the *whole* dictionary? Almost a *million* words? Why do you believe him or disbelieve him?

Suppose Malcolm X actually did exactly what he says he did. To judge only from what you read of his words in this exercise, what would you say his motivation for copying the dictionary was? Would you call his motives admirable? Complex? You will be speculating here, of course, but not just airily supposing; you will be looking, that is, at how you move from words to meaning in Malcolm X's sentences.

It is clear that Malcolm X did not want to write as he talked: "How would I sound writing in slang?" How would he have sounded, and why do you suppose he wasn't satisfied to sound as he thought he would have? Isn't naturalness a virtue?

What do you think Malcolm X did want to sound like? A Theme-writer? The New York Public Library? Any other possibilities?

In addition to copying out the dictionary, Malcolm X suggests that he also read aloud what he had written "over and over." And he sees a connection between these activities and his becoming articulate, a writer and a speaker. (Perhaps with no more than an eighth grade education he was ignorant of what is said to have happened in the world since 1872 or thereabouts?) Do you think that such activities did help him to become a writer? A speaker? What makes you say so, one way or the other?

But suppose someone who knew for sure told you that Malcolm X never became The Writer He Wanted To Be. (Who does?) Suppose you accepted the observation. What then would you say was the effect of the actions involved in his copying out the dictionary? What exactly did Malcolm X rote-learn, anyway? Words? Definitions? The Dictionary? Anything else?

Now, what about you and your education in the light of this description of a learning experience? Can you imagine yourself doing such a thing as copying out the dictionary under any circumstances? Have you ever done anything like that? Have you ever known anyone or of anyone other than Malcolm X who did? With what results? Can you imagine any benefit to your doing such a thing? Any detriment? When it comes to an understanding of such terms as "dictionary," "copying," "read back aloud," and "words," what similarities are there between you and Malcolm X? What are the differences?

*   *   *

N.B. It will be assumed that when you come to class to discuss this assignment you will know who Malcolm X was and know also something about his life, his career, and what he stood for. Be ready to furnish specific information on your references. Hearsay, word-of-mouth information, will not be acceptable. For what reason do you suppose?

12. Benjamin Franklin (Part I)

In his *Autobiography*, Benjamin Franklin tells of his dropping formal attendance at the Presbyterian church. He was in his mid-twenties at the time and had been what might be called today a "good Presbyterian" for most of his life. But he had been growing increasingly dissatisfied with not receiving from the Sunday services "the kind of good things that [he] expected." He was particularly disappointed in the sermons he heard, which he describes as "chiefly either polemic arguments or explications of the peculiar doctrines of our sect. To me [they were] very dry, uninteresting, and unedifying, since not a single moral principle was inculcated or enforced, their aim seeming to be rather to make us Presbyterians than good citizens."

Such windy Sundays came once too often, and though Franklin continued throughout his life to support the church as an institution by paying his annual subscription (he also made donations for the founding of other churches), he "went no more to the public assemblies." Franklin continues:

It was about this time [that] I conceived the bold and arduous project of arriving at moral perfection. I wished to live without committing any fault at any time; I would conquer all that either natural inclination, custom, or company might lead me into. As I knew, or thought I knew, what was right and wrong, I did not see why I might not always do the one and avoid the other. But I soon found I had undertaken a task of more difficulty than I had imagined. While my care was employed in guarding against one fault, I was often surprised by another; habit took the advantage of inattention; inclination was sometimes too strong for reason. I concluded, at length, that the mere speculative conviction that it was to our interest to be completely virtuous, was not sufficient to prevent our slipping; and that the contrary habits must be broken, and good ones acquired and established, before we can have any dependence on a steady, uniform rectitude of conduct. For this purpose I therefore contrived the following method.

In the various enumerations of the moral virtues I had met with in my reading, I found the catalogue more or less numerous, as different writers included more or fewer ideas under the same name. Temperance, for example, was by some confined to eating and drinking, while by others it was extended to mean the moderating of every other pleasure, appetite, inclination or passion, bodily or mental, even to our avarice and ambition. I proposed to myself for the sake of clearness, to use rather more names, with fewer ideas annexed to each, than a few names with more ideas; and I included under thirteen names of virtues all that at that time occurred to me as necessary or desirable, and annexed to each a short precept, which fully expressed the extent I gave to its meaning.

These names of virtues, with their precepts, were:

1. *Temperance*—Eat not to dullness; drink not to elevation.
2. *Silence*—Speak not but what may benefit others or yourself; avoid trifling conversation.
3. *Order*—Let all your things have their places; let each part of your business have its time.
4. *Resolution*—Resolve to perform what you ought; perform without fail what you resolve.
5. *Frugality*—Make no expense but to do good to others or yourself; i.e., waste nothing.
6. *Industry*—Lose no time; be always employed in something useful; cut off all unnecessary actions.
7. *Sincerity*—Use no hurtful deceit; think innocently and justly, and if you speak, speak accordingly.
8. *Justice*—Wrong none by doing injuries, or omitting the benefits that are your duty.
9. *Moderation*—Avoid extremes; forbear resenting injuries so much as you think they deserve.
10. *Cleanliness*—Tolerate no uncleanliness in body, clothes, or habitation.
11. *Tranquility*—Be not disturbed at trifles, or at accidents common or unavoidable.
12. *Chastity*—Rarely use venery but for health or offspring, never to dullness, weakness, or the injury of your own or another's peace or reputation.
13. *Humility*—Imitate Jesus and Socrates.

My intention being to acquire the *habitude* of all these virtues, I judged it would be well not to distract my attention by attempting the whole at once, but to fix it on one of them at a time; and, when I should be master of that, then to proceed to another, and so on, till I should have gone through the thirteen; and, as the previous acquisition of some might facilitate the acquisition of certain others, I arranged them with that view, as they stand above. Temperance first, as it tends to procure that coolness and clearness of head, which is so necessary where constant vigilance was to be kept up, and guard maintained against the unremitting attraction of ancient habits, and the force of perpetual temptations. This being acquired and established *Silence* would be more easy; and my desire being to gain knowledge at the same time that I improved in virtue, and considering that in conversation it was obtained rather by the use of the ears than of the tongue, and therefore wishing to break a habit I was getting into of prattling, punning, and joking, which only made me acceptable to trifling company, I gave *Silence* the second place. This and the next, *Order,* I expected would allow me more time for attending to my project and my studies. *Resolution,* once become habitual, would keep me firm in my endeavors to obtain all the subsequent virtues; *Frugality* and *Industry* freeing me from my remaining debt, and producing affluence and independence, would make more easy the practice of *Sincerity* and *Justice,* etc., etc. Conceiving then, that, agreeably to the advice of Pythagoras in his Golden Verses, daily examination would be necessary, I contrived the following method for conducting that examination.

I made a little book, in which I allotted a page for each of the virtues. I ruled each page with red ink, so as to have seven columns, one for each day of the week, marking each column with a letter for the day. I crossed these columns with thirteen red lines, marking the beginning of each line with the first letter of one of the virtues, on which line, and in its proper column, I might mark, by a little black spot, every fault I found upon examination to have been committed respecting that virtue upon that day.

I determined to give a week's strict attention to each of the virtues successively. Thus, in the first week, my great guard was to avoid every day the least offence against *Temperance,* leaving the other virtues to their ordinary chance, only marking every evening the faults of the day. Thus, if in the first week I could keep my first line, marked T, clear of spots, I supposed the habit of that virtue so much strengthened, and its opposite weakened, that I might venture extending my attention to include the next, and for the following week keep both lines clear of spots. Proceeding thus to the last, I could go through a course complete in thirteen weeks, and four courses in a year. And like him who, having a garden to weed, does not attempt to eradicate all the bad herbs at once, which would exceed his reach and his strength, but works on one of the beds at a time, and, having accomplished the first, proceeds to a second, so I should have, I hoped, the encouraging pleasure of seeing on my pages the progress I made in virtue, by clearing successively my lines of their spots, till in the end, by a number of courses, I should be happy in viewing a clean book, after a thirteen weeks' daily examination.

—Benjamin Franklin *

* From *The Autobiography of Benjamin Franklin,* The Pocket Library, 1954, pp. 102–105.

The section of the *Autobiography* that we are concerned with here was written in 1784. Franklin was 79.

*   *   *

Franklin's scheme for self-development is based on certain assumptions about how he works as a human being, about the nature of human character. What are these assumptions? What is it he thought he could learn? What does he seem to think he can know?

Evidently, Franklin left off attending church less in anger than with a sense of disappointment. In what exactly? What did Franklin seem to think that a church should do? What does he mean, for example, by implying that moral principles should be both "inculcated" and "enforced?" What does he mean by a term such as "good citizens"?

Look over the list of virtues and their definitions. Reread what Franklin says about how he constructed it. Do you really think he did all that reading, all that selecting and modifying? What makes you say so?

What do you make of those virtues and their definitions? Are these just Pieties? Abstractions? Or can you infer anything more particular from them about the sort of man Franklin was? Perhaps it might help here for you to imagine what a list for yourself would look like.

Franklin explains why he arranged the virtues in the order he did. What do you understand from this explanation? Is there anything you do not understand from it?

The method Franklin contrived for conducting his daily examination involved him in the specific activity of making marks on paper (a form of writing?). Does this strike you as carrying things a bit too far? Couldn't he have kept score in his head, for example? Why do you suppose that Franklin seemed to think this specific daily activity was necessary?

Franklin says that in working at his project he was surprised to find himself "fuller of faults" than he imagined (what with all his markings and erasures, for example, he wore out that first "little book" and had to make himself another—with leaves of vellum the second time, not paper). But he goes on to say that he had "the satisfaction of seeing [his faults] diminish." Do you believe this?

Who would be the ideal audience for Benjamin Franklin? Characterize this audience as completely as you can.

Once again, examine the issues here in the light of your own life and experience. Have you ever set a project for yourself of the sort that Franklin did? Did the possibility ever occur to you? How do you account for the fact that it did or didn't? Does Franklin's project have anything to offer you? And how do you know? Be sure you explain what you mean by "project" here.

* * *

N.B. Again, it is assumed that you will know something of the life and character of Benjamin Franklin when you come to class and that you will be able to supply written sources for your information.

13. *Benjamin Franklin (Part II)*

Franklin follows the account of his scheme of self-development with the following:

> It may be well my posterity should be informed that to this little artifice, with the blessing of God, their ancestor owed the constant felicity of his life, down to his 79th year, in which this is written. What reverses may attend the remainder is in the hand of Providence; but, if they arrive, the reflection on past happiness enjoyed ought to help his bearing them with more resignation. To Temperance he ascribes his long-continued health, and what is still left to him of a good constitution; to Industry and Frugality, the early easiness of his circumstances and acquisition of his fortune, with all that knowledge that enabled him to be a useful citizen, and obtained for him some degree of reputation among the learned; to Sincerity and Justice, the confidence of his country: and the honorable employs it conferred upon him; and to the joint influence of the whole mass of the virtues, even in the imperfect state he was able to acquire them, all that evenness of temper, and that cheerfulness in conversation, which makes his company still sought for, and agreeable even to his younger acquaintance. I hope, therefore, that some of my descendants may follow the example and reap the benefits.
>
> *—Benjamin Franklin* *

What do you make of such a way of talking, all those capital letters, for example; that pronoun shift ("my posterity"; "his 79th year") and back again ("I hope")?

When you compare the benefits which Franklin "ascribes" to his virtues above with the way he defines those same virtues in his original list, how would you describe the difference between what he seems to have hoped he would get from working on them and what he seems to have got?

How do you characterize the voice you hear speaking to you in the passage? What sort of tone does it have?

Are you being asked something in such a passage? Told something? Taught something? Or what exactly? And what is your response to what you hear?

* Ibid., p. 111.

Return to the question of whether or not you believe that Franklin saw his faults "diminish." Does the passage above influence your belief one way or another? Why?

Return also to the question of whether Franklin's project has anything to offer you. Is your stand on such a question the same as it was? How do you account for this? Do you understand the term "project" the way you first did? Why?

14. D. H. Lawrence

D. H. Lawrence in his *Studies in Classic American Literature* devotes a chapter to Benjamin Franklin and has this to say about his scheme of self-development:

> I am a moral animal. But I am not a moral machine. I don't work with a little set of handles or levers. The temperance-silence-order - resolution - frugality - industry - sincerity - justice - moderation - cleanliness-tranquillity-chastity-humility keyboard is not going to get me going. I'm really not just an automatic piano with a moral Benjamin getting tunes out of me.*

And then Lawrence, too, develops a list:

1. *Temperance*—Eat and carouse with Bacchus, or munch dry bread with Jesus, but don't sit down without one of the gods.
2. *Silence*—Be still when you have nothing to say; when genuine passion moves you, say what you've got to say, and say it hot.
3. *Order*—Know that you are responsible to the gods inside you and to the men in whom the gods are manifest. Recognize your superiors and your inferiors, according to the gods. This is the root of all order.
4. *Resolution*—Resolve to abide by your own deepest promptings, and to sacrifice the smaller thing to the greater. Kill when you must, and be killed the same: the must coming from the gods inside you, or from the men in whom you recognize the Holy Ghost.
5. *Frugality*—Demand nothing; accept what you see fit. Don't waste your pride or squander your emotion.
6. *Industry*—Lose no time with ideals; serve the Holy Ghost; never serve mankind.
7. *Sincerity*—To be sincere is to remember that I am I, and that the other man is not me.
8. *Justice*—The only justice is to follow the sincere intuition of the soul, angry or gentle. Anger is just, and pity is just, but judgment is never just.
9. *Moderation*—Beware of absolutes. There are many gods.
10. *Cleanliness*—Don't be too clean. It impoverishes the blood.

* From *Studies in Classic American Literature* by D. H. Lawrence. Copyright © 1923, 1951 by Frieda Lawrence, © 1961 by the Estate of the late Frieda Lawrence. Reprinted by permission of The Viking Press, Inc.

11. *Tranquility*—The soul has many motions, many gods come and go. Try and find your deepest issue, in every confusion, and abide by that. Obey the man in whom you recognize the Holy Ghost; command when your honour comes to command.
12. *Chastity*—Never "use" venery at all. Follow your passional impulse, if it be answered in the other being; but never have any motive in mind, neither offspring nor health nor even pleasure, nor even service. Only know that "venery" is of the great gods. An offering-up of yourself to the very great gods, the dark ones, and nothing else.
13. *Humility*—See all men and women according to the Holy Ghost that is within them. Never yield before the barren.

There's my list. I have been trying dimly to realize it for a long time, and only America and old Benjamin have at last goaded me into trying to formulate it. And now I, at least, know why I can't stand Benjamin. He tries to take away my wholeness and my dark forest, my freedom. For how can any man be free, without an illimitable background? And Benjamin tries to shove me into a barbed wire paddock and make me grow potatoes or Chicagoes.

And how can I be free, without gods that come and go? But Benjamin won't let anything exist except my useful fellow men, and I'm sick of them; as for his Godhead, his Providence, He is Head of nothing except a vast heavenly store that keeps every imaginable line of goods, from victrolas to cat-o'-nine tails.

*   *   *

Lawrence's essay on Franklin is also predicated on certain assumptions about what it means to be a human being, about what is learnable, what is knowable. Trace out these assumptions. How do they compare with what you see as Franklin's assumptions about the way in which people are people? The following are for the purpose of helping you to locate yourself with these questions.

Look over Lawrence's list of virtues. What do you make of his definitions of Franklin's terms? Are these definitions clear? Do you understand, for example, what Lawrence means by "the gods" (of whom Bacchus and Jesus seem to be two)? How about "the Holy Ghost"? You have, presumably, seen such terms before.

Lawrence also makes use of terms for which you may have no immediate context: "the dark ones," "my dark forest." What do you make of them?

If you find yourself unable to supply equivalents for some of Lawrence's terms, if you cannot translate into your own language the concept of sexuality, say, that seems to underlie what Lawrence says of *Chastity,* then does that mean that you have no idea of what he is talking about? Would you feel right saying that Lawrence is simply incomprehensible? Or can you, out of the corner of your eye, see the possibility of another way of talking here?

What do you think Lawrence is doing in his essay on Franklin? Is he attacking him? Is he trying to teach something? Who would make up the ideal audience for D. H. Lawrence?

Does Lawrence have anything to offer you? Are his assumptions about the nature of human character your assumptions? Or do you disagree with him? Are you comfortable in your agreement or disagreement? Why?

*   *   *

N.B. Once more, as you found out about Malcolm X and Benjamin Franklin, find out about D. H. Lawrence by the time you come to class.

15. The Perfect Student

This diagram of the Perfect Student was constructed by a teacher of composition who was annoyed with the way in which his students chose to describe themselves. (Annoyed with what, do you suppose?)

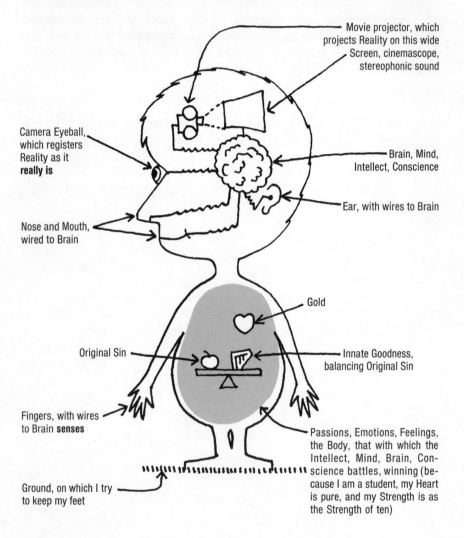

Diagram of the Perfect Student (After a diagram by John F. Butler)

It is really a diagram of a number of commonly used metaphors placed within a simple plan of the human body. The result is laughable, yet there is some meaning conveyed by the diagram which we can recognize. We do speak of someone's heart of gold and we do describe the nervous system as if it were an electronic device. That is, under certain circumstances we are inclined to talk this way.

* * *

According to the details of the diagram, how does this Perfect Student operate? How does he go about learning? What can he know? Would he be able to copy out the dictionary as Malcolm X did? Could he construct and follow a project of the sort devised by Benjamin Franklin? Would he be able to look at Franklin's scheme for self-improvement as D. H. Lawrence did? Perhaps, and if you'd like equal time, you could address these questions by devising a diagram of the Perfect Teacher for this Perfect Student, or by attempting to imagine the Perfect Educational Institution for him.

When you compare yourself as a student with this diagram of the Perfect Student, what do you find? Have you ever behaved as though you believed you were the Perfect Student? Would there be any advantages to someone's doing so? Would there be any disadvantages?

But of course you are not the Perfect Student. How are you different? Is it going to be enough to claim, as the Perfect Student might, that you think, or that you are an Individual? How do you see yourself as the student you think you are? What metaphors do you have for how you operate, for what you want to learn, to know? Are you not as good as the Perfect Student? Better off? Simply different? Or what, exactly?

16. S. H. Hadley

Here is another account of what can be seen as a learning experience:

One Tuesday evening I sat in a saloon in Harlem, a homeless, friendless, dying drunkard. I had pawned or sold everything that would bring a drink. I could not sleep unless I was dead drunk. I had not eaten for days, and for four nights preceding I had suffered with delirium tremens, or the horrors, from midnight till morning. I had often said, "I will never be a tramp. I will never be cornered, for when that time comes, if ever it comes, I will find a home in the bottom of the river." But the Lord so ordered it that when that time did come I was not able to walk one quarter of the way to the river. As I sat there thinking, I seemed to feel some great and mighty presence. I did not know then what it was. I did learn afterwards that it was Jesus, the sinner's friend. I walked up to the bar and pounded it with my fist till I made the glasses rattle. Those who stood by drinking looked on with scornful curiosity. I said I would never take another drink, if I died on the street, and really I felt as though that would happen before morning. Something said, "If you want to keep this promise, go and have yourself locked up." I went to the nearest station-house and had myself locked up.

I was placed in a narrow cell, and it seemed as though all the demons that could find room came in that place with me. This was not all the company I had, either. No, praise the Lord; that dear Spirit that came to me in the saloon was present, and said, Pray. I did pray, and though I did not feel any great help, I kept on praying. As soon as I was able to leave my cell I was taken to the police court and remanded back to the cell. I was finally released, and found my way to my brother's house, where every care was given me. While lying in bed the admonishing Spirit never left me, and when I arose the following Sabbath morning I felt that day would decide my fate, and toward evening it came into my head to go to Jerry M'Auley's Mission. I went. The house was packed, and with great difficulty I made my way to the space near the platform. There I saw the apostle to the drunkard and the outcast —that man of God, Jerry M'Auley. He rose, and amid deep silence told [of] his experience [as a drunkard and of his recovery from alcoholism through a belief in Christ]. There was a sincerity about this man that carried conviction with it, and I found myself saying, "I wonder if God can save me?" I listened to the testimony of twenty-five or thirty persons every one of whom had been saved from rum, and I made up my mind that I would be saved or die right there. When the invitation was given, I knelt down with a crowd of drunkards. Jerry made the first prayer. Then Mrs. M'Auley prayed fervently for us. Oh, what a conflict was going on for my poor soul! A blessed whisper said, "Come"; the devil said, "Be careful." I halted but a moment, and then, with a breaking heart, I said, "Dear Jesus, can you help me?" Never with mortal tongue can I describe that moment. Although up to that moment my soul had been filled with indescribable gloom, I felt the glorious brightness of the noonday sun shine into my heart. I felt I was a free man. Oh, the precious feeling of safety, of freedom, of resting on Jesus! I felt that Christ with all his brightness and power had come into my life; that, indeed, old things had passed away and all things had become new.

From that moment till now I have never wanted a drink of whiskey, and I have never seen money enough to make me take one. I promised God that night that if he would take away that appetite for strong drink, I would work for him all my life. He has done his part, and I have been trying to do mine.*

That Hadley was a drunkard who quite suddenly became sober and to the end of his life never touched alcohol again is a matter of record. William James, who quotes Hadley's account of himself in his *Varieties of Religious Experience,* says that after his conversion he became "an active and useful rescuer of [other] drunkards in New York."

This is an account of what is sometimes called a conversion experience. One state of mind or being is exchanged for another. To judge from what Hadley has written, where would you locate the moment of his change of mind, of his conversion? What brings the change about? What is this mind that Hadley changes? From what to what does he change it?

The following are intended to help you locate yourself in addressing these questions.

Hadley sees the talk of Jerry M'Auley as crucial to his change of mind, his conversion. Yet it is difficult to believe that Hadley had not heard of Jesus Christ before his meeting with M'Auley. Why do you think that M'Auley's talk seems to have made the difference to him that it did?

You will remember from your experience with Assignment 4 that once you change your mind it is hard to recall what your previous state of mind had been, what it was you changed from, how you could ever not know what is now so plain, how you could ever not see what is now right before your eyes. Does Hadley seem to have any difficulty recalling

---

* S. H. Hadley, *Rescue Mission Work,* Old Jerry M'Auley Water Street Mission, New York, 1890.

his previous state of mind? With what terminology does he organize his state of mind before his conversion, for example? Is there a difference between that terminology and the terminology with which he organizes his present? His future?

So far as Hadley's future is concerned, he did indeed become, as James says, "an active and useful rescuer of [other] drunkards." Like M'Auley, his way of becoming active was to tell his own story. At mission meeting after mission meeting he repeated it and repeated it and repeated it. (Perhaps, as Malcolm X seems to have been, Hadley was ignorant of what has happened in the world since 1872 or thereabouts?) Whatever effect this activity of Hadley's may have had on others, what effect do you imagine it might have had on him?

It would, of course, be possible for someone other than Hadley to explain what happened to him another way, with another set of terms. How might a Freudian explain Hadley's experience, for example? Or a Jungian? Or an atheist? How and for whom might the use of another set of terms for explaining Hadley's experience be beneficial? How and for whom might the same set of other terms be other than beneficial?

Hadley himself might have chosen to explain what happened to him another way, with another set of terms. Suppose, for example, he chose to call that "great and mighty presence" a hallucination? Suppose he had chosen to see what went on at M'Auley's as hokum? What differences, exactly, would such changes in terminology have made? Is not a rose a rose by any name?

"We learn from our experience." You are familiar with the proverbial connection. "Experience is the best teacher." But what kind of talk is this? You have for example, experienced the telephone dial in full detail and recently. But can you say for sure right now at what letter the lettering order on the dial reverses itself? (On the other hand, you might feel on safer ground with the little dot at the center of the dialing holes?) Similarly, when you notice the various ways in which what happened to Hadley can be talked about, does it seem accurate to say that it was from his *experience* that Hadley learned? What then did he learn from? What saved him from drink?

17. A Madman

The passage below is quoted by William James in a section of *Varieties of Religious Experience,* subtitled "The Sick Soul" (Modern Library Edition, pp. 145–146). It is a letter written by an inmate of a mental institution, a patient for whom James says "the sun has left his heaven" (p. 146). James's book (the full title of which is *The Varieties of Religious Experience: A Study in Human Nature*) was first published in 1902.

I suffer too much in this hospital, both physically and morally. Besides the burnings and the sleeplessness (for I no longer sleep since I am shut up here, and the little rest I get is broken by bad dreams, and I am waked with a jump by nightmares, dreadful visions, lightning, thunder, and the rest), fear, atrocious fear, presses me down, holds me without respite, never lets me go. Where is the justice in it all! What have I done to deserve this excess of severity? Under what form will this fear crush me? What would I not owe to any one who would rid me of my life! Eat, drink, lie awake all night, suffer without interruption—such is the fine legacy I have received from my mother! What I fail to understand is this abuse of power. There are limits to everything, there is a middle way. But God knows neither middle way nor limits. I say God, but why? All I have known so far has been the devil. After all, I am afraid of God as much as of the devil, so I drift along, thinking of nothing but suicide, but with neither courage nor means here to execute the act. As you read this, it will easily prove to you my insanity. The style and the ideas are incoherent enough—I can see that myself. But I cannot keep myself from being either crazy or an idiot; and, as things are, from whom should I ask pity? I am defenseless against the invisible enemy who is tightening his coils around me. I should be no better armed against him even if I saw him, or had seen him. Oh, if he would but kill me, devil take him! Death, death, once for all! But I stop. I have raved to you long enough. I say raved, for I can write no otherwise, having neither brain nor thoughts left. O God! what a misfortune to be born! Born like a mushroom, doubtless between an evening and a morning; and how true and right I was when in our philosophy-year in college I chewed the cud of bitterness with the pessimists. Yes, indeed, there is more pain in life than gladness—it is one long agony until the grave. Think how gay it makes me to remember that this horrible misery of mine, coupled with this unspeakable fear, may last fifty, one hundred, who knows how many more years!

First of all, the voice you hear speaking in the passage is not totally unfamiliar to you, is it? Not to you, not to anyone. Why? Where and under what circumstances have you heard something like that voice before? What is familiar about what you hear in the passage? But the way you hear that voice in other circumstances is not the way you hear it here. Why not?

Malcolm X, Franklin, D. H. Lawrence, and S. H. Hadley in their attempts to become more than they were, may all be said to have developed languages, or ways of seeing themselves and their experience, that enabled them to assume responsibility for the shapes of their own lives, to grow, to belong to themselves. To judge from what he has written, the writer of the passage above has also told himself about his experience in order to establish a relationship with it. What is this relationship exactly? With what terms does he organize the world he lives in? How does he define these terms? To what end is the process directed?

Project yourself into a position that it is no exaggeration to say you may someday find yourself in. Assume that the statement above represents a state of mind for which you have chosen to accept some reponsibility. How would you characterize the speaker of that passage for yourself? As mentally disturbed? As faking? Explain what you would mean by whatever terms you think you would choose. Do you think your choice of terms would make a difference?

What would you say or do in the face of this phenomenon that you have chosen to accept some responsibility for? Would you talk to the speaker? How? What would you say? Or would your talking do no good? Would talking itself do no good? What do you think would help the speaker of the passage? Jesus? (meaning what exactly?) Psychiatric Treatment? (which would involve?)

18. A Good Teacher

The evaluation of a teacher's effectiveness as a teacher is a complicated business. "Teacher" and "effective" mean different things to different people. The terms can also mean different things at different times to the same person. A generally agreed upon unit of measure, therefore, is difficult to come by. A standard scale is difficult to come by.

What is true for the evaluator of a teacher is no less true of the teacher himself. Every teacher does some things well and other things not so well. And like his students, every teacher has good days and bad days. Every teacher is a person as well as a teacher—with all that that implies.

Here, for example, is an account of a teacher by one of his former students:

> Dr. Albert Thomas Carter died on 29th July. . . . He was 85; and was the most individual and pungent Tutor [1] in the House [2] from 1895 to 1923. To sum up his contradictions in proper perspective is not easy. With his long, lean, legal, Mephistophelian face and beautiful elocution, he was as memorable for his reading of the Lessons in Cathedral [3] as for his highly polished and often luridly startling stories, and for his well-known aphorisms: "live and let die"; "self not service"; "anything to give pain"; "the best is good enough for me." . . . His intellect was brilliant—cool, sharp, and ruthless; he had got Firsts in Mods and Greats, [4] the Eldon and the Vinerian, [5] and had lectured for long as Reader in Constitutional Law and Legal History at the Inns of Court: [6] and he was the author of two crisp and lucid legal books. For potential Firsts and Blues, [7] the common objects of academic snobbery in aging Tutors, he was a magnificent teacher; with idlers his methods could be the more horrifying for their inhuman and sardonic suavity; if they would

---

[1] In English universities, a college official in charge of the studies of an undergraduate.
[2] Christ Church, Oxford.
[3] Reading of scripture in chapel.
[4] Honors in intermediate examinations and classics.
[5] Endowed professorships.
[6] The four voluntary legal societies in England which have the exclusive right to call candidates to the English bar, after they have received such instruction and taken such examinations as the Inns stipulate and provide. A Reader is a lecturing professor.
[7] Honor students and varsity athletes.

not try, neither would he, except to make things unpleasant for them. He was by nature easily tolerant and benevolent, and to his friends a constant but anxious joy, and he won their real affection. But to the dim and weakly he could be unpardonably and odiously cruel, and he was irascible at games. When Albany [8] was bombed, he moved for a time to Queen's, his old College, which had made him an Honorary Fellow; he didn't mind danger in London, he said, but could not bear discomfort. But he was a highly critical and unaccommodating war-time lodger, and at last returned to Albany and to a sadly solitary existence made worse by failing sight. His collection of silver was superb; and when to add to it became too costly even for him, he made a splendid collection of English gold coins, which he said were cheaper. . . . To cheerful youth, as he loved to call it, "The Don" was a great figure; his entertainments were memorable; and he was worldly wise to a degree unusual in dons. Friendly, ribald, shocking, loyal, sociable, difficult, and infinitely amusing, he inspired affection and rage with equal apparent indifference. He was like nobody else in his virtues and defects; but in a big S.C.R.[9] his failings mattered less; one forgets his occasional brutalities, and thinks of him now with real tenderness, not untouched with awe.

—Roger Venables *

This obituary is the work of Robert H. Dundas, the subject of Venables's book. It was published in a printed letter, corresponding to what we would call the alumni news, sent to former students at Christ Church (a college of Oxford University).

*　　*　　*

How would you characterize Dundas's attitudes toward Dr. Carter as a teacher? Would you call the passage sentimental? Nostalgic? Or what exactly? Would you call it admiring?

Whatever you think Dundas may think of Dr. Carter as a teacher, does he display anything in his writing that you think he might have learned from working under him?

What kind of a teacher would you call Dr. Carter? Do you think that you could learn anything from such a teacher? How do you know?

[8] A residence in London.
[9] Senior Common Room: a group made up of the head and faculty of a College.
* From *"D" Portrait of a Don* by Roger Venables, Oxford, 1967, p. 128ff. Reprinted by permission of Basil Blackwell Publisher.

*　　*　　*

Whatever the basis of your evaluation of the teachers you have had in the past, you have certainly had, at some time or other, a teacher you think of as good.

Choose a teacher from your experience that you would call a good teacher, one from whom you believe you learned something, and write a paper in which you show what's good about him, so far as you're concerned. What made him or makes him a good teacher? The key word here is "show." What did this teacher do, exactly? What did you do? What came of this doing? Perhaps you could write this paper as though it were a scene in a short story, a particular scene in which particular people move and speak.

Finally, look back at what you have written in your paper. Note particularly any metaphors you may have used to explain this teaching-learning process. What exactly have you defined?

19. *Wilder and Agassiz*

Here is another example of a student remembering one of his former teachers:

Agassiz handled all specimens with the greatest care, and naturally had little patience with clumsiness. . . . At one of the lectures he had handed down for inspection a very rare and costly fossil, from the coal-measures, I think; including the matrix, it had about the size and shape of the palm of the hand. He cautioned us not to drop it. When it had reached about the middle of the audience a crash was heard. The precious thing had been dropped by a new and somewhat uncouth assistant whom we will call Dr. X. He hastily gathered up the pieces and rushed out of the room. For a few seconds Agassiz stood as if himself petrified; then, without even an "Excuse me," he vanished by the same door. Presently he returned, flushed, gazing ruefully at the fragments in his hand, covered with mucilage or liquid glue. After a pause, during which those who knew him not awaited an explosive denunciation of gaucherie, Agassiz said quietly: "In natural history it is not enough to know how to study specimens; it is also necessary to know how to handle them"—and then proceeded with his lecture.

—Burt G. Wilder *

One sentence from the passage above has been omitted (see ellipses). The form of it is: "The following incident illustrates both his _____ _____ [two words] and his _____ [one word]." From what you have of the passage to work with, determine what you can of what Wilder seems to think of Agassiz as a teacher, and then, just for fun, try to supply the missing three words. Why do you choose the terms you do?

Now choose three words which seem to imply something different from the words you think that Wilder may have used. How can the account be read so as to justify this second set of words as those that Wilder may have used?

What does the fact that two such readings are possible enable you to conclude about Agassiz as a teacher, about Wilder as a student, about the nature of the teaching-learning process? What did Agassiz do? What did Wilder do? What came of this doing?

* Burt G. Wilder, "Louis Agassiz, Teacher," *The Harvard Graduate Magazine,* June, 1907, pp. 47–48.

20. Shaler and Agassiz

Here is another estimate of Louis Agassiz as a teacher. Again, the writer is one of his former students, N. S. Shaler, who studied zoology under Agassiz as an undergraduate at Harvard and later became a Professor of Geology at the same University. The passage is taken from *The Autobiography of Nathaniel Southgate Shaler.*

When I sat me down before my tin pan, Agassiz brought me a small fish, placing it before me with the rather stern requirement that I should study it, but should on no account talk to any one concerning it, nor read anything relating to fishes, until I had his permission so to do. To my inquiry, "What shall I do?" he said in effect: "Find out what you can without damaging the specimen; when I think that you have done the work I will question you." In the course of an hour I thought I had compassed that fish; it was rather an unsavory object, giving forth the stench of old alcohol, then loathsome to me, though in time I came to like it. Many of the scales were loosened so that they fell off. It appeared to me to be a case for a summary report, which I was anxious to make and get on to the next stage of the business. But Agassiz, though always within call, concerned himself no further with me that day, nor the next, nor for a week. At first, this neglect was distressing; but I saw that it was a game, for he was, as I discerned rather than saw, covertly watching me. So I set my wits to work upon the thing, and in the course of a hundred hours or so thought I had done much—a hundred times as much as seemed possible at the start. I got interested in finding out how the scales went in series, their shape, the form and placement of the teeth, etc. Finally, I felt full of the subject, and probably expressed it in my bearing; as for words about it then, there were none from my master except his cheery "Good morning." At length, on the seventh day, came the question, "Well?" and my disgorge of learning to him as he sat on the edge of my table puffing his cigar. At the end of the hour's telling, he swung off and away, saying: "That is not right." Here I began to think that, after all, perhaps the rules for scanning Latin verse were not the worst infliction in the world. Moreover, it was clear that he was playing a game with me to find if I were capable of doing hard, continuous work without the support of a teacher, and this stimulated me to labor. I went at the task anew, discarded my first notes, and in another week of ten hours a day labor I had results which astonished myself and satisfied him. Still there was no trace of praise in words or manner. He signified that it would do by placing before me about a half a peck of bones, telling me to see what I could make of them, with no further directions to guide me. I soon found that they were the skeletons of half a dozen fishes of different species; the jaws told me so much at a first inspection. The task evidently was to fit the separate bones together in their proper order. Two months or more went to this task with no other help than an occasional looking over my grouping with the stereotyped remark: "That is not right." Finally, the task was done, and I was again set upon alcoholic specimens—this time a remarkable lot of specimens representing, perhaps, twenty species of the side-swimmers or Pleuronectidae.

I shall never forget the sense of power in dealing with things which I felt in beginning the more extended work on a group of animals. I had learned the art of comparing objects, which is the basis of the naturalist's work. At this stage I was allowed to read, and to discuss my work with others about me. I did both eagerly, and acquired a considerable knowledge of the literature of ichthyology, becoming especially interested in the system of classification, then most imperfect. I tried to follow Agassiz's scheme of division into the order of ctenoids and ganoids, with the result that I found one of my species of side-swimmers had cycloid scales on one side and ctenoid on the other. This not only shocked my sense of the value of classification in a way that permitted of no full recovery of my original respect for the process, but for a time shook my confidence in my master's knowledge. At the same time I had a malicious pleasure in exhibiting my "find" to him expecting to repay in part the humiliation which he had evidently tried to inflict on my conceit. To my question as to how the nondescript should be classified he said: "My boy, there are now two of us who know that."

At the time of the events narrated by Shaler (1859–1860) there were no written examinations on any subjects to be taken by candidates for the Scientific School (as the College of Science at Harvard was then called). Admission to a course of study was by permission of the professors in charge of the several departments who questioned candidates orally in order to determine their fitness to proceed for a degree. The students who were accepted paid their fees directly to their teachers who depended on such additions to their salaries in order to live. (In 1859, for example, Agassiz was paid only $2,500 a year in salary by the University, a sum that Shaler himself calls "meager.") "Few or none," Shaler remarks, "who had any semblance of an education" were denied admission to Agassiz's laboratory." But a number of those granted admission stayed there a good deal longer than the four years required for a degree. For Agassiz refused to recommend the graduation of "some who had been with him for many years, and had succeeded in their special work, giving as reason for his denial that they were 'too ignorant.' " Shaler recalls that the preliminary examination Agassiz gave him "was directed first to find that I knew enough Latin and Greek to make use of those languages." Then came a test in German and French. He seemed not at all interested, Shaler states, "to find what I knew about fossils, rocks, animals and plants"—at which the student was, of course, "offended." On the day that Shaler sat him down before that tin pan, Agassiz's laboratory consisted of "one room about thirty feet long and fifteen feet wide" the whole of which was invariably "packed" with students. The rest of the "two story building" was given over to storerooms in which Agassiz's "collections were crammed." In this, his second meeting with Agassiz, Shaler was simply assigned a place at "a small pine table." The tin pan before him he remembers distinctly as being very rusty.

What did Shaler learn from Agassiz so far as you are concerned? Locate as specifically as you can some instances of this learning. What sentences and terms do you go to? What do you say that this learning consists of?

Is what Shaler seems to think he learned from Agassiz the same thing that Agassiz taught him? Is what he seems to think he learned the same thing as what he did learn? What does Shaler seem to think of Agassiz as a teacher?

Where do you find yourself with Agassiz as a teacher, with the whole process of teaching and learning as it was conducted in 1859–60 or thereabouts? Can you imagine electing to study under such a man in such a system? How would you respond to a teacher who made it very clear to you that you would need his "permission" to read about a subject, or who told you after you had worked for seven days on something simply that what you had done wasn't "right"? What would you think of a physics teacher who used your ability to write a sentence in English as a gauge for your fitness to study physics? How would you respond to a teacher with "no trace of praise in words or manner"? Or would it depend? On what? Are you accustomed to seeing teachers as out to inflict humiliation on your conceit? Is that a right you are accustomed to grant them? Or do you have another way of understanding the process of teaching and learning?

And what about those working conditions, the rusty equipment, everybody crammed into one room of a two story house the rest of which was made into storerooms for Agassiz's collections? Would you resent a comparable situation in your own education? To judge from what Shaler says above, how do you imagine he saw the conditions under which he worked? (Just by the way, the omitted sentence from the passage by Wilder given you on the last assignment reads as follows: "The following incident illustrates both his kindly spirit and his self-restraint.") When you compare yourself as a student with Shaler what similarities do you find? Any differences?

*   *   *

N.B.   When you come to class know who Louis Agassiz was and, again, be able to supply the printed source or sources for your information.

21. Teaching and Learning: A Situation

Here is a sketch that involves the subject of learning:

"Man, I remember something when I was little, a boy," somebody named Lee says. He is hunched forward, his elbows on the table, a tumbler of wine between his hands. "About a dog. Little miserable dog of mine."

"Yeah, man, go on," Mike says, his eyes lighting up.

"I get up real early to do my paper route. Los Angeles *Examiner*," Lee says. "Streets always empty, just a few milk trucks and bakery trucks and other kids like me. My dog goes along, see? Every day he trots along with me. Little mongrel dog."

"Yeah, yeah, go on, man," Mike says, impatient for the story, sure that it has meaning.

"There we are in all those big empty streets. Just me and the dog. Sun coming up, papers falling on the porches, me dreaming and walking and the dog trotting," Lee says. "Then far away, about as big as a black mosquito, I see this hopped-up Model A. Wonderful pipes on it, blatting so sweet I could hear them for six blocks. I stand there on the curb, listening to that sweet sound and watching that car come weaving down that empty street. And the dog stands in the gutter, watching too. That Model A gets bigger and I can see the chrome pipes on the side, the twin Strombergs sucking air, just eating up the asphalt."

He pauses and Mike leans forward and says urgently, "Now man, come on, go. I wanna hear this."

"This Model A is a roadster and there is a Mexican driving and his girl with him," Lee says slowly, stalking the climax. "It weaves across the street, and me and the dog stare at it. And it comes for us in a big slow curve and hit that dog. His back broke in mid-air and he was dead when he hit the street again. Like a big man cracking a seed in his teeth . . . same sound, I mean. And the girl stares back at me and laughs. And I laugh. You see why, man?"

The two of them sit quietly, looking down at the wine and listening to the jazz. Mike glances once at Lee and then back at his glass. He has learned something secret and private about Lee, and that is good enough. After a while they sit back, smiling, and listen to the jazz.

—Eugene Burdick *

* Eugene Burdick, "The Innocent Nihilists Adrift in Squaresville," *The Reporter*, April 1958, p. 33. Reprinted by permission of Curtis Brown, Ltd. Copyright © 1958 by Eugene Burdick.

Burdick shapes his account in such a way as to cast Lee in the conventional role of teacher, Mike in the conventional role of student. What sort of teacher does Burdick seem to think that Lee is? What sort of student does he seem to think Mike is? To judge from your understanding of what Burdick has written, what does he seem to think is taught on this occasion? What is learned?

In a sense, Burdick the writer is also a teacher. We his readers are students. In presenting the relationship between Lee and Mike as he does here, what does Burdick teach about teaching and learning? What meaning do you as a reader-student make of Burdick's teaching?

22. *A Flash of Insight*

Here is an account of an act of learning:

. . . Edison created the phonograph in a single day in 1877. Years before . . . a phenomenon occurred while he was experimenting upon the idea of sending a telegraph signal from a whirling disc upon which a stylus pricked electromagnetic embossed telegraphic dots and dashes, creating a musical hum when the disc whirled at high speed. In 1877 he developed a funnel-like toy. When he talked through the funnel, the vibrations caused by his voice worked a pawl which turned a ratchet wheel connected by a pulley with a paper figure of a man operating a paper saw on a paper log. Edison noted that at times the man moved rhythmically, at times jerkily, depending upon the words shouted at the horn and the pitch of his voice. Out of the setting of the musical hum, noted years previously, and the industrious paper man sawing his paper log came the *flash of insight* which produced a phonograph in thirty hours.

—Austin L. Porterfield *

At one time or another you have certainly had what is referred to above as a "flash of insight." When you look back over your experience, you can isolate a moment of illumination, of things coming together so that as it turned out, you had an idea, saw a solution, knew what to do.

See if you can recapture such a moment and put it on paper. The resulting "new idea" may not really be a very new idea at all. Yet it was good enough for you at the moment and you took some satisfaction in it.

On the basis of what you have written, what would you say is involved in a "flash of insight"? What exactly got put together with what? What was the result of this putting together?

---

* From *Creative Factors in Scientific Research* by Austin L. Porterfield, Duke University Press, 1941, p. 95. Reprinted by permission of Duke University Press.

23. Writing as Learning

This assignment gives you the opportunity to define the development of a piece of writing and to conclude what you can about the meaning of the process.

Like you, the writer of the versions of the paper reproduced here was a student in a composition course. The first version of the paper was required. That is, it was a paper written to address a specific writing assignment. The second and third versions the writer did on her own. The assignment read as follows:

> We often say in this course that a writer ought to write about what he knows. Let us assume for the sake of this paper that one thing all of us know is this school and its surroundings. We are speaking now of the school in terms of its physical thereness, its location and arrangement as a place.
>
> Describe some part of Drexel University as you see it. The emphasis here is on both the word "see" and the word "you." That is, take care that you don't swallow up the scene with metaphor, but try to make what you see an image of what *you* see (not of what just anybody could see). Perhaps you would find it most fruitful to work with something about which you have some ambiguity of attitude, about which you feel more than one way. Try also to avoid obvious cop-outs: "The cafeteria at lunchtime is certainly a scene of varied activity," etc.

The following pages show the three versions of the paper.

Here is the first version of the paper as marked by the teacher:

~~The beauty of the Asbury church~~ comes from its con-
~~trasts. From its appearance on the outside, I would not~~
~~suspect that it had any~~ connection with Drexel--in other
The Asbury Church is
~~words, it's~~ not made of orange brick. It is a big, solid-
looking, old building. ~~This~~ oldness is one of the quali-
ties that appeals to me. In comparison with the rest of
the University area, the uniform, "modern" architecture,
Asbury has character and stability.

Let a reader say this.

→ *Now go on so that a reader can say "Its beauty is its contrast. It's unlike the rest of Drexel," etc.*

Inside the building in the sanctuary is the same
atmosphere. It is a huge room, with a ceiling two stories
up, lined with stained glass windows, (the picture of an
old-fashioned church.

This is the tip-off that you're working with clichés.

And yet what goes on inside is anything but old-
fashioned. The service is <u>creative</u> and bears almost no
resemblance to a <u>normal</u>, conventional service. The min-
isters are <u>young</u> and <u>interested</u> in the Universities and
the community. There are projects aimed at actively attacking some of the <u>problems</u> in Philadelphia.

Can't you hear how these are close-out terms -generalizations that bury what you see?

Possibly my reaction is a form of rebellion, although
one I won't admit to. The church I attended before coming
to Philadelphia is a typical suburban church--a small
the building is?
redwood building that is <u>fairly</u> well landscaped, and has
a standard service. While Asbury is old-fashioned and
slightly crumbling, it is also very now.

Again--do the scene so that the scene says this.

With control the metaphor might work.

Here is the second version as marked:

The Asbury Church is not made of orange brick. It is an old stone building.

There are rows and rows of long pews, with designs carved in the wood. Probably 400 people could attend, although 40 is a crowd. The stained glass windows are big; they fill the walls. Very bright colors echo on the floor.

These details don't seem pointed enough.

Underneath so much stillness is a lot of activity that can't be seen. Only occasionally do the sounds of the people staying in the weekend shelter downstairs make their way up here into the sanctuary. Some of those people are wearing awfully old, unmatched clothes, and they don't look clean and happy and thankful as like you're supposed to in a church.

And? Can you extend the ambiguity here or fill it out?

The organ fills a large corner, as if the pipes are growing there. They look too big, almost. The ceiling is so far away, in is you... almost forgotten. It encloses the room--the area, but only in that it shuts out the outside; it adds to the feeling of space. ¶? There are always enormous areas that are motionless.

There's not enough precision in the finish here for me. Maybe you need some suggestion of your having re-seen the church?

60 *Composing*

Here is the third version:

Unlike the rest of Drexel, the Asbury Church is not made of orange brick. It is an old, beautifully fitted stone building.

There are rows and rows of long pews, all of them with designs carved deep in the black wood. Probably 400 people could attend a service, although most Sundays 40 is a crowd. The stained glass windows seem to have swallowed the walls. The sun throws its bright colors into pleasant patterns on the floor. Most of the time, even on Sundays, it is very, very still.

Underneath the stillness is a lot of activity that can't be seen. But only occasionally do the sounds of the people staying in the weekend shelter downstairs make their way up here into the sanctuary. Most of the people down there wear old, unmatched clothes. They don't look clean and happy and thankful the way you're supposed to look in a church. A lot of them are activists of one sort or another. They share their meals.

The organ fills a large corner looking as if its pipes are growing there. They look too big, almost. The ceiling is so far away you almost forget about it. It encloses things but only in that it shuts out the outside; inside it adds to the feeling of space. There are always enormous areas of motionlessness. Sometimes the quiet seems almost dead still.

One way of preparing yourself to address the following questions might be to imagine how you would mark the third version of this paper if you were the teacher of this student in this course. (We are speaking of more here than the assigning of a grade.) Suppose that in addition to your marginalia, you felt compelled to write a final comment on the paper. What would it be? What would you expect the student to understand by it?

How would you describe what it is that seems to happen from version to version of this paper? From what to what does the paper move, exactly? How would you evaluate this movement? Does the student have anything at the end of the process that she didn't have at the beginning of it? How about the teacher?

What part did the teacher play in the process? What did he do?

What part did the student play in the process? What did *she* do?

On the basis of what you have said so far, define "teacher" in the development of this piece of writing. Then define "student."

24. Why Doesn't Education Work Better?

Even with the best will in the world, and no matter how experienced or skilled they may be, teachers do not always teach. Nor do students, even when they are intelligent, highly-motivated, well-prepared, etc., always learn.

What's the trouble here? Why doesn't an educational institution work better than it does? Why doesn't education work better than it does—even when everyone wants it to?

Address these questions by examining your relation to your own learning at the educational institution you are attending. What are the fundamental difficulties you encounter even when you want to learn, even when you make up your mind to work at it? What would you say are the greatest barriers to your learning inside an educational institution?

Can you think of any alternatives to the system of formal education as you know it? Another system? The abolition of institutionalized education altogether?

25. Lewis Padgett

The following science fiction story may be read as a statement about the relationship of teaching and learning as processes of language.

Mimsy Were the Borogoves

by Lewis Padgett *

There's no use trying to describe either Unthahorsten or his surroundings, because, for one thing, a good many million years had passed since 1942 Anno Domini, and, for another, Unthahorsten wasn't on Earth, technically speaking. He was doing the equivalent of standing in the equivalent of a laboratory. He was preparing to test his time machine.

Having turned on the power, Unthahorsten suddenly realized that the Box was empty. Which wouldn't do at all. The device needed a control, a three-dimensional solid which would react to the conditions of another age. Otherwise Unthahorsten couldn't tell, on the machine's return, where and when it had been. Whereas a solid in the Box would automatically be subject to the entropy and cosmic ray bombardment of the other era, and Unthahorsten could measure the changes, both qualitative and quantitative, when the machine returned. The Calculators could then get to work and, presently, tell Unthahorsten that the Box had briefly visited 1,000,000 A.D., 1,000 A.D., or 1 A.D., as the case might be.

Not that it mattered, except to Unthahorsten. But he was childish in many respects.

There was little time to waste. The Box was beginning to glow and shiver. Unthahorsten stared around wildly, fled into the next glossatch, and groped in a storage bin there. He came up with an armful of peculiar-looking stuff. Uh-huh. Some of the discarded toys of his son Snowen, which the boy had brought with him when he had passed over from Earth, after mastering the necessary technique. Well, Snowen needed this junk no longer. He was conditioned, and had put away childish things. Besides, though Unthahorsten's wife kept the toys for sentimental reasons, the experiment was more important.

* First published in 1943 ("Lewis Padgett" was a pseudonym employed by Henry Kuttner and his wife, C. L. Moore). Copyright © 1954 by Lewis Padgett. Reprinted by permission of Harold Matson Co., Inc.

Unthahorsten left the glossatch and dumped the assortment into the Box, slamming the cover shut just before the warning signal flashed. The Box went away. The manner of its departure hurt Unthahorsten's eyes.

He waited.

And he waited.

Eventually he gave up and built another time machine, with identical results. Snowen hadn't been annoyed by the loss of his old toys, nor had Snowen's mother, so Unthahorsten cleaned out the bin and dumped the remainder of his son's childhood relics in the second time machine's Box.

According to his calculations, this one should have appeared on Earth, in the latter part of the nineteenth century, A.D. If that actually occurred, the device remained there.

Disgusted, Unthahorsten decided to make no more time machines. But the mischief had been done. There were two of them, and the first—

Scott Paradine found it while he was playing hooky from the Glendale Grammar School. There was a geography test that day, and Scott saw no sense in memorizing place names—which in 1942 was a fairly sensible theory. Besides, it was the sort of warm spring day, with a touch of coolness in the breeze, which invited a boy to lie down in a field and stare at the occasional clouds till he fell asleep. Nuts to geography! Scott dozed.

About noon he got hungry, so his stocky legs carried him to a nearby store. There he invested his small hoard with penurious care and a sublime disregard for his gastric juices. He went down by the creek to feed.

Having finished his supply of cheese, chocolate, and cookies, and having drained the soda-pop bottle to its dregs, Scott caught tadpoles and studied them with a certain amount of scientific curiosity. He did not persevere. Something tumbled down the bank and thudded into the muddy ground near the water, so Scott, with a wary glance around, hurried to investigate.

It was a box. It was, in fact, the Box. The gadgetry hitched to it meant little to Scott, though he wondered why it was so fused and burnt. He pondered. With his jackknife he pried and probed, his tongue sticking out from a corner of his mouth—Hm-m-m. Nobody was around. Where had the box come from? Somebody must have left it here, and sliding soil had dislodged it from its precarious perch.

"That's a helix," Scott decided, quite erroneously. It was helical, but it wasn't a helix, because of the dimensional warp involved. Had the thing been a model airplane, no matter how complicated, it would have held few mysteries to Scott. As it was, a problem was posed. Something told Scott that the device was a lot more complicated than the spring motor he had deftly dismantled last Friday.

But no boy has ever left a box unopened, unless forcibly dragged away. Scott probed deeper. The angles on this thing were funny. Short circuit, probably. That was why—*uh!* The knife slipped. Scott sucked his thumb and gave vent to experienced blasphemy.

Maybe it was a music box.

Scott shouldn't have felt depressed. The gadgetry would have given Einstein a headache and driven Steinmetz raving mad. The trouble was, of course, that the box had not yet completely entered the space-time continuum where Scott existed, and therefore it could not be opened. At any rate, not till Scott used a convenient rock to hammer the helical non-helix into a more convenient position.

He hammered it, in fact, from its contact point with the fourth dimension, releasing the space-time torsion it had been maintaining. There was a brittle snap. The box jarred slightly, and lay motionless, no longer only partially in existence. Scott opened it easily now.

The soft, woven helmet was the first thing that caught his eye, but he discarded that without much interest. It was just a cap. Next he lifted a square, transparent crystal block, small enough to cup in his palm—much too small to contain the maze of apparatus within it. In a moment Scott had solved that problem. The crystal was a sort of magnifying glass, vastly enlarging the things inside the block. Strange things they were, too. Miniature people, for example—

They moved. Like clockwork automatons, though much more smoothly. It was rather like watching a play. Scott was interested in their costumes, but fascinated by their actions. The tiny people were deftly building a house. Scott wished it would catch fire, so he could see the people put it out.

Flames licked up from the half-completed structure. The automatons, with a great deal of odd apparatus, extinguished the blaze.

It didn't take Scott long to catch on. But he was a little worried. The manikins would obey his thoughts. By the time he discovered that, he was frightened, and threw the cube from him.

Halfway up the bank, he reconsidered and returned. The crystal block lay partly in the water, shining in the sun. It was a toy; Scott sensed that, with the unerring instinct of a child. But he didn't pick it up immediately. Instead, he returned to the box and investigated its remaining contents.

He found some really remarkable gadgets. The afternoon passed all too quickly. Scott finally put the toys back in the box and lugged it home, grunting and puffing. He was quite red-faced by the time he arrived at the kitchen door.

His find he hid at the back of a closet in his own room upstairs. The crystal cube he slipped into his pocket, which already bulged with string, a coil of wire, two pennies, a wad of tinfoil, a grimy defense stamp, and a chunk of feldspar. Emma, Scott's two-year-old sister, waddled unsteadily in from the hall and said hello.

"Hello, Slug," Scott nodded, from his altitude of seven years and some months. He patronized Emma shockingly, but she didn't know the difference. Small, plump, and wide-eyed, she flopped down on the carpet and stared dolefully at her shoes.

"Tie 'em, Scotty, please?"

"Sap," Scott told her kindly, but knotted the laces. "Dinner ready yet?"

Emma nodded.

"Let's see your hands." For a wonder they were reasonably clean, though probably not aseptic. Scott regarded his own paws thoughtfully and, grimacing, went to the bathroom, where he made a sketchy toilet. The tadpoles had left traces.

Dennis Paradine and his wife Jane were having a cocktail before dinner, downstairs in the living room. He was a youngish, middle-aged man with gray-shot hair and a thinnish, prim-mouthed face; he taught philosophy at the university. Jane was small, neat, dark, and very pretty. She sipped her Martini and said:

"New shoes. Like 'em?"

"Here's to crime," Paradine muttered absently. "Huh? Shoes? Not now. Wait till I've finished this. I had a bad day."

"Exams?"

"Yeah. Flaming youth aspiring toward manhood. I hope they die. In considerable agony. *Insh'Allah!*"

"I want the olive," Jane requested.

"I know," Paradine said despondently. "It's been years since I've tasted one myself. In a Martini, I mean. Even if I put six of 'em in your glass, you're still not satisfied."

"I want yours. Blood brotherhood. Symbolism. That's why."

Paradine regarded his wife balefully and crossed his long legs. "You sound like one of my students."

"Like that hussy Betty Dawson, perhaps?" Jane unsheathed her nails. "Does she still leer at you in that offensive way?"

"She does. The child is a neat psychological problem. Luckily she isn't mine. If she were—" Paradine nodded significantly. "Sex consciousness and too many movies. I suppose she still thinks she can get a passing grade by showing me her knees. Which are, by the way, rather bony."

Jane adjusted her skirt with an air of complacent pride. Paradine uncoiled himself and poured fresh Martinis. "Candidly, I don't see the point of teaching those apes philosophy. They're all at the wrong age. Their habit-patterns, their methods of thinking, are already laid down.

They're horribly conservative, not that they'd admit it. The only people who can understand philosophy are mature adults or kids like Emma and Scotty."

"Well, don't enroll Scotty in your course," Jane requested. "He isn't ready to be a *Philosophiae Doctor*. I hold no brief for child geniuses, especially when it's my son."

"Scotty would probably be better at it than Betty Dawson," Paradine grunted.

" 'He died an enfeebled old dotard at five,' " Jane quoted dreamily. "I want your olive."

"Here. By the way, I like the shoes."

"Thank you. Here's Rosalie. Dinner?"

"It's all ready, Miz Pa'dine," said Rosalie, hovering. "I'll call Miss Emma 'n' Mista' Scotty."

"I'll get 'em." Paradine put his head into the next room and roared, "Kids! Come and get it!"

Small feet scuttered down the stairs. Scott dashed into view, scrubbed and shining, a rebellious cowlick aimed at the zenith. Emma pursued, levering herself carefully down the steps. Halfway she gave up the attempt to descend upright and reversed, finishing the task monkey-fashion her small behind giving an impression of marvelous diligence upon the work in hand. Paradine watched, fascinated by the spectacle, till he was hurled back by the impact of his son's body.

"Hi, dad!" Scott shrieked.

Paradine recovered himself and regarded Scott with dignity. "Hi, yourself. Help me in to dinner. You've dislocated at least one of my hip joints."

But Scott was already tearing into the next room, where he stepped on Jane's new shoes in an ecstasy of affection, burbled an apology, and rushed off to find his place at the dinner table. Paradine cocked up an eyebrow as he followed, Emma's pudgy hand desperately gripping his forefinger.

"Wonder what the young devil's been up to?"

"No good, probably," Jane sighed. "Hello, darling. Let's see your ears."

"They're *clean*. Mickey licked 'em."

"Well, that Airedale's tongue is far cleaner than your ears," Jane pondered, making a brief examination. "Still, as long as you can hear, the dirt's only superficial."

"Fisshul?"

"Just a little, that means." Jane dragged her daughter to the table and inserted her legs into a high chair. Only lately had Emma graduated to the dignity of dining with the rest of the family, and she was, as Paradine remarked, all eat up with pride by the prospect. Only babies spilled food, Emma had been told. As a result, she took such painstaking care in conveying her spoon to her mouth that Paradine got the jitters whenever he watched.

"A conveyer belt would be the thing for Emma," he suggested, pulling out a chair for Jane. "Small buckets of spinach arriving at her face at stated intervals."

Dinner proceeded uneventfully until Paradine happened to glance at Scott's plate. "Hello, there. Sick? Been stuffing yourself at lunch?"

Scott thoughtfully examined the food still left before him. "I've had all I need, dad," he explained.

"You usually eat all you can hold, and a great deal more," Paradine said. "I know growing boys need several tons of foodstuff a day, but you're below par tonight. Feel O.K.?"

"Uh-huh. Honest, I've had all I need."

"All you *want?*"

"Sure. I eat different."

"Something they taught you at school?" Jane inquired.

Scott shook his head solemnly.

"Nobody taught me. I found it out myself. I use spit."

"Try again," Paradine suggested. "It's the wrong word."

"Uh . . . s-saliva. Hm-m-m?"

"Uh-huh. More pepsin? Is there pepsin in the salivary juices, Jane? I forget."

"There's poison in mine," Jane remarked. "Rosalie's left lumps in the mashed potatoes again."

But Paradine was interested. "You mean you're getting everything possible out of your food—no wastage—and eating less?"

Scott thought that over. "I guess so. It's not just the sp . . . saliva. I sort of measure how much to put in my mouth at once, and what stuff to mix up. I dunno. I just do it."

"Hm-m-m," said Paradine, making a note to check up later. "Rather a revolutionary idea." Kids often get screwy notions, but this one might not be so far off the beam. He pursed his lips. "Eventually I suppose people will eat quite differently—I mean the *way* they eat, as well as what. What they eat, I mean. Jane, our son shows signs of becoming a genius."

"Oh?"

"It's a rather good point in dietetics he just made. Did you figure it out yourself, Scott?"

"Sure," the boy said, and really believed it.

"Where'd you get the idea?"

"Oh, I—" Scott wriggled. "I dunno. It doesn't mean much, I guess."
Paradine was unreasonably disappointed. "But surely—"

"S-s-s-spit!" Emma shrieked, overcome by a sudden fit of badness.
"Spit!" she attempted to demonstrate, but succeeded only in dribbling into
her bib.

With a resigned air Jane rescued and reproved her daughter, while
Paradine eyed Scott with rather puzzled interest. But it was not till after
dinner, in the living room, that anything further happened.

"Any homework?"

"N-no," Scott said, flushing guiltily. To cover his embarrassment he
took from his pocket a gadget he had found in the box, and began to un-
fold it. The result resembled a tesseract, strung with beads. Paradine
didn't see it at first, but Emma did. She wanted to play with it.

"No. Lay off, Slug," Scott ordered. "You can watch me." He fumbled
with the beads, making soft, interested noises. Emma extended a fat
forefinger and yelped.

"Scotty," Paradine said warningly.

"I didn't hurt her."

"Bit me. It did," Emma mourned.

Paradine looked up. He frowned, staring. What in—

"Is that an abacus?" he asked. "Let's see it, please."

Somewhat unwillingly Scott brought the gadget across to his father's
chair. Paradine blinked. The "abacus," unfolded, was more than a foot
square, composed of thin, rigid wires that interlocked here and there. On
the wires the colored beads were strung. They could be slid back and
forth, and from one support to another, even at the points of jointure.
But—a pierced bead couldn't cross *interlocking* wires—

So, apparently, they weren't pierced. Paradine looked closer. Each
small sphere had a deep groove running around it, so that it could be
revolved and slid along the wire at the same time. Paradine tried to pull
one free. It clung as though magnetically. Iron? It looked more like
plastic.

The framework itself—Paradine wasn't a mathematician. But the angles
formed by the wires were vaguely shocking, in their ridiculous lack of
Euclidean logic. They were a maze. Perhaps that's what the gadget was—
a puzzle.

"Where'd you get this?"

"Uncle Harry gave it to me," Scott said on the spur of the moment.
"Last Sunday, when he came over." Uncle Harry was out of town, a cir-
cumstance Scott well knew. At the age of seven, a boy soon learns that
the vagaries of adults follow a certain definite pattern, and that they are
fussy about the donors of gifts. Moreover, Uncle Harry would not return

for several weeks; the expiration of that period was unimaginable to Scott, or, at least, the fact that his lie would ultimately be discovered meant less to him than the advantages of being allowed to keep the toy.

Paradine found himself growing slightly confused as he attempted to manipulate the beads. The angles were vaguely illogical. It was like a puzzle. This red bead, if slid along *this* wire to *that* junction, should reach *there*—but it didn't. A maze, odd, but no doubt instructive. Paradine had a well-founded feeling that he'd have no patience with the thing himself.

Scott did, however, retiring to a corner and sliding beads around with much fumbling and grunting. The beads *did* sting, when Scott chose the wrong ones or tried to slide them in the wrong direction. At last he crowed exultantly.

"I did it, dad!"

"Eh? What? Let's see." The device looked exactly the same to Paradine, but Scott pointed and beamed.

"I made it disappear."

"It's still there."

"That blue bead. It's gone now."

Paradine didn't believe that, so he merely snorted. Scott puzzled over the framework again. He experimented. This time there were no shocks, even slight. The abacus had showed him the correct method. Now it was up to him to do it on his own. The bizarre angles of the wires seemed a little less confusing now, somehow.

It was a most instructive toy—

It worked, Scott thought, rather like the crystal cube. Reminded of that gadget, he took it from his pocket and relinquished the abacus to Emma, who was struck dumb with joy. She fell to work sliding the beads, this time without protesting against the shocks—which, indeed, were very minor—and, being imitative, she managed to make a bead disappear almost as quickly as had Scott. The blue bead reappeared— but Scott didn't notice. He had forethoughtfully retired into an angle of the chesterfield with an overstuffed chair and amused himself with the cube.

There were little people inside the thing, tiny manikins much enlarged by the magnifying properties of the crystal, and they moved, all right. They built a house. It caught fire, with realistic-seeming flames, and stood by waiting. Scott puffed urgently. "Put it *out!*"

But nothing happened. Where was that queer fire engine, with revolving arms, that had appeared before? Here it was. It came sailing into the picture and stopped. Scott urged it on.

This was fun. Like putting on a play, only more real. The little people did what Scott told them, inside of his head. If he made a mistake, they waited till he'd found the right way. They even posed new problems for him—

The cube, too, was a most instructive toy. It was teaching Scott, with alarming rapidity—and teaching him very entertainingly. But it gave him no really new knowledge as yet. He wasn't ready. Later—later—

Emma grew tired of the abacus and went in search of Scott. She couldn't find him, even in his room, but once there the contents of the closet intrigued her. She discovered the box. It contained treasure-trove —a doll, which Scott had already noticed but discarded with a sneer. Squealing, Emma brought the doll downstairs, squatted in the middle of the floor, and began to take it apart.

"Darling! What's that?"

"Mr. Bear!"

Obviously it wasn't Mr. Bear, who was blind, earless, but comforting in his soft fatness. But all dolls were named Mr. Bear to Emma.

Jane Paradine hesitated. "Did you take that from some other little girl?"

"I didn't. She's mine."

Scott came out from his hiding place, thrusting the cube into his pocket. "Uh—that's from Uncle Harry."

"Did Uncle Harry give that to you, Emma?"

"He gave it to me for Emma," Scott put in hastily, adding another stone to his foundation of deceit. "Last Sunday."

"You'll break it, dear."

Emma brought the doll to her mother. "She comes apart. See?"

"Oh? It . . . *ugh!*" Jane sucked in her breath. Paradine looked up quickly.

"What's up?"

She brought the doll over to him, hesitated, and then went into the dining room, giving Paradine a significant glance. He followed, closing the door. Jane had already placed the doll on the cleared table.

"This isn't very nice, is it, Denny?"

"Hm-m-m." It was rather unpleasant, at first glance. One might have expected an anatomical dummy in a medical school, but a child's doll—

The thing came apart in sections, skin, muscles, organs, miniature but quite perfect, as far as Paradine could see. He was interested. "Dunno. Such things haven't the same connotations to a kid—"

"Look at that liver. Is it a liver?"

"Sure. Say, I . . . this is funny."

"What?"

"It isn't anatomically perfect, after all." Paradine pulled up a chair.

"The digestive tract's too short. No large intestine. No appendix, either."

"Should Emma have a thing like this?"

"I wouldn't mind having it myself," Paradine said. "Where on earth did Harry pick it up? No, I don't see any harm in it. Adults are conditioned to react unpleasantly to innards. Kids don't. They figure they're solid inside, like a potato. Emma can get a sound working knowledge of physiology from this doll."

"But what are those? Nerves?"

"No, these are the nerves. Arteries here; veins here. Funny sort of aorta—" Paradine looked baffled. "That . . . what's Latin for network? Anyway . . . huh? *Rita? Rata?*"

"*Rales,*" Jane suggested at random.

"That's a sort of breathing," Paradine said crushingly. "I can't figure out what this luminous network of stuff is. It goes all through the body, like nerves."

"Blood."

"Nope. Not circulatory, not neural—funny! It seems to be hooked up with the lungs."

They became engrossed, puzzling over the strange doll. It was made with remarkable perfection of detail, and that in itself was strange, in view of the physiological variation from the norm. "Wait'll I get that Gould," Paradine said, and presently was comparing the doll with anatomical charts. He learned little, except to increase his bafflement.

But it was more fun than a jigsaw puzzle.

Meanwhile, in the adjoining room, Emma was sliding the beads to and fro in the abacus. The motions didn't seem so strange now. Even when the beads vanished. She could almost follow that new direction—almost—

Scott panted, staring into the crystal cube and mentally directing, with many false starts, the building of a structure somewhat more complicated than the one which had been destroyed by fire. He, too, was learning—being conditioned—

Paradine's mistake, from a completely anthropomorphic standpoint, was that he didn't get rid of the toys instantly. He did not realize their significance, and, by the time he did, the progression of circumstances had got well under way. Uncle Harry remained out of town, so Paradine couldn't check with him. Too, the midterm exams were on, which meant arduous mental effort and complete exhaustion at night; and Jane was slightly ill for a week or so. Emma and Scott had free rein with the toys.

"What," Scott asked his father one evening, "is a wabe, dad?"

"Wave?"

He hesitated. "I . . . don't *think* so. Isn't wabe right?"

"Wab is Scot for web. That it?"

"I don't see how," Scott muttered, and wandered off, scowling, to amuse himself with the abacus. He was able to handle it quite deftly now. But, with the instinct of children for avoiding interruptions, he and Emma usually played with the toys in private. Not obviously, of course —but the more intricate experiments were never performed under the eye of an adult.

Scott was learning fast. What he now saw in the crystal cube had little relationship to the original simple problems. But they were fascinatingly technical. Had Scott realized that his education was being guided and supervised—though merely mechanically—he would probably have lost interest. As it was, his initiative was never quashed.

Abacus, cube, doll—and other toys the children found in the box—

Neither Paradine nor Jane guessed how much of an effect the contents of the time machine were having on the kids. How could they? Youngsters are instinctive dramatists, for purposes of self-protection. They have not yet fitted themselves to the exigencies—to them partially inexplicable—of a mature world. Moreover, their lives are complicated by human variables. They are told by one person that playing in the mud is permissible, but that, in their excavations, they must not uproot flowers or small trees. Another adult vetoes mud *per se*. The Ten Commandments are not carved on stone; they vary, and children are helplessly dependent on the caprice of those who give them birth and feed and clothe them. And tyrannize. The young animal does not resent that benevolent tyranny, for it is an essential part of nature. He is, however, an individualist, and maintains his integrity by a subtle, passive fight.

Under the eyes of an adult he changes. Like an actor on-stage, when he remembers, he strives to please, and also to attract attention to himself. Such attempts are not unknown to maturity. But adults are less obvious—to other adults.

It is difficult to admit that children lack subtlety. Children are different from the mature animal because they think in another way. We can more or less easily pierce the pretenses they set up—but they can do the same to us. Ruthlessly a child can destroy the pretenses of an adult. Iconoclasm is their prerogative.

Foppishness, for example. The amenities of social intercourse, exaggerated not quite to absurdity. The gigolo—

"Such *savoir faire!* Such punctilious courtesy!" The dowager and the blond young thing are often impressed. Men have less pleasant comments to make. But the child goes to the root of the matter.

"You're *silly!*"

How can an immature human understand the complicated system of social relationships? He can't. To him, an exaggeration of natural courtesy is silly. In his functional structure of life-patterns, it is rococo. He is an egotistic little animal, who cannot visualize himself in the position of another—certainly not an adult. A self-contained, almost perfect natural unit, his wants supplied by others, the child is much like a unicellular creature floating in the blood stream, nutriment carried to him, waste products carried away—

From the standpoint of logic, a child is rather horribly perfect. A baby may be even more perfect, but so alien to an adult that only superficial standards of comparison apply. The thought processes of an infant are completely unimaginable. But babies think, even before birth. In the womb they move and sleep, not entirely through instinct. We are conditioned to react rather peculiarly to the idea that a nearly-viable embryo may think. We are surprised, shocked into laughter, and repelled. Nothing human is alien.

But a baby is not human. An embryo is far less human.

That, perhaps, was why Emma learned more from the toys than did Scott. He could communicate his thoughts, of course; Emma could not, except in cryptic fragments. The matter of the scrawls, for example—

Give a young child pencil and paper, and he will draw something which looks different to him than to an adult. The absurd scribbles have little resemblance to a fire engine, but it *is* a fire engine, to a baby. Perhaps it is even three-dimensional. Babies think differently and see differently.

Paradine brooded over that, reading his paper one evening and watching Emma and Scott communicate. Scott was questioning his sister. Sometimes he did it in English. More often he had resource to gibberish and sign language. Emma tried to reply, but the handicap was too great.

Finally Scott got pencil and paper. Emma liked that. Tongue in cheek, she laboriously wrote a message. Scott took the paper, examined it, and scowled.

"That isn't right, Emma," he said.

Emma nodded vigorously. She seized the pencil again and made more scrawls. Scott puzzled for a while, finally smiled rather hesitantly, and got up. He vanished into the hall. Emma returned to the abacus.

Paradine rose and glanced down at the paper, with some mad thought that Emma might abruptly have mastered calligraphy. But she hadn't. The paper was covered with meaningless scrawls, of a type familiar to any parent. Paradine pursed his lips.

It might be a graph showing the mental variations of a manic-depressive cockroach, but probably wasn't. Still, it no doubt had meaning to Emma. Perhaps the scribble represented Mr. Bear.

Scott returned, looking pleased. He met Emma's gaze and nodded. Paradine felt a twinge of curiosity.

"Secrets?"

"Nope. Emma . . . uh . . . asked me to do something for her."

"Oh." Paradine, recalling instances of babies who had babbled in unknown tongues and baffled linguists, made a note to pocket the paper when the kids had finished with it. The next day he showed the scrawl to Elkins at the university. Elkins had a sound working knowledge of many unlikely languages, but he chuckled over Emma's venture into literature.

"Here's a free translation, Dennis. Quote. I don't know what this means, but I kid the hell out of my father with it. Unquote."

The two men laughed and went off to their classes. But later Paradine was to remember the incident. Especially after he met Holloway. Before that, however, months were to pass, and the situation to develop even further toward its climax.

Perhaps Paradine and Jane had evinced too much interest in the toys. Emma and Scott took to keeping them hidden, playing with them only in private. They never did it overtly, but with a certain unobtrusive caution. Nevertheless, Jane especially was somewhat troubled.

She spoke to Paradine about it one evening. "That doll Harry gave Emma."

"Yeah?"

"I was downtown today and tried to find out where it came from. No soap."

"Maybe Harry bought it in New York."

Jane was unconvinced. "I asked them about the other things, too. They showed me their stock—Johnsons's a big store, you know. But there's nothing like Emma's abacus."

"Hm-m-m." Paradine wasn't much interested. They had tickets for a show that night, and it was getting late. So the subject was dropped for the nonce.

Later it cropped up again, when a neighbor telephoned Jane.

"Scotty's never been like that, Denny. Mrs. Burns said he frightened the devil out of her Francis."

"Francis? A little fat bully of a punk, isn't he? Like his father. I broke Burns' nose for him once, when we were sophomores."

"Stop boasting and listen," Jane said, mixing a highball. "Scott showed Francis something that scared him. Hadn't you better—"

"I suppose so." Paradine listened. Noises in the next room told him the whereabouts of his son. "Scotty!"

"Bang," Scott said, and appeared smiling. "I killed 'em all. Space pirates. You want me, dad?"

"Yes. If you don't mind leaving the space pirates unburied for a few minutes. What did you do to Francis Burns?"

Scott's blue eyes reflected incredible candor. "Huh?"

"Try hard. You can remember, I'm sure."

"Uh. Oh, that. I didn't do nothing."

"Anything," Jane corrected absently.

"Anything. Honest. I just let him look into my television set, and it . . . it scared him."

"Television set?"

Scott produced the crystal cube. "It isn't really that. See?"

Paradine examined the gadget, startled by the magnification. All he could see, though, was a maze of meaningless colored designs.

"Uncle Harry—"

Paradine reached for the telephone. Scott gulped. "Is . . . is Uncle Harry back in town?"

"Yeah."

"Well, I gotta take a bath." Scott headed for the door. Paradine met Jane's gaze and nodded significantly.

Harry was home, but disclaimed all knowledge of the peculiar toys. Rather grimly, Paradine requested Scott to bring down from his room all of the playthings. Finally they lay in a row on the table, cube, abacus, doll, helmetlike cap, several other mysterious contraptions. Scott was cross-examined. He lied valiantly for a time, but broke down at last and bawled, hiccuping his confession.

"Get the box these things came in," Paradine ordered. "Then head for bed."

"Are you . . . hup! . . . gonna punish me, daddy?"

"For playing hooky and lying, yes. You know the rules. No more shows for two weeks. No sodas for the same period."

Scott gulped. "You gonna keep my things?"

"I don't know yet."

"Well . . . g'night, daddy. G'night, mom."

After the small figure had gone upstairs, Paradine dragged a chair to the table and carefully scrutinized the box. He poked thoughtfully at the fused gadgetry. Jane watched.

"What is it, Denny?"

"Dunno. Who'd leave a box of toys down by the creek?"

"It might have fallen out of a car."

"Not at that point. The road doesn't hit the creek north of the railroad trestle. Empty lots—nothing else." Paradine lit a cigarette. "Drink, honey?"

"I'll fix it." Jane went to work, her eyes troubled. She brought Paradine a glass and stood behind him, ruffling his hair with her fingers. "Is anything wrong?"

"Of course not. Only—where did these toys come from?"

"Johnsons's didn't know, and they get their stock from New York."

"I've been checking up, too," Paradine admitted. "That doll"—he poked it—"rather worried me. Custom jobs, maybe, but I wish I knew who'd made 'em."

"A psychologist? The abacus—don't they give people tests with such things?"

Paradine snapped his fingers. "Right! And say! There's a guy going to speak at the university next week, fellow named Holloway, who's a child psychologist. He's a big shot, with quite a reputation. He might know something about it."

"Holloway? I don't—"

"Rex Holloway. He's . . . hm-m-m! He doesn't live far from here. Do you suppose he might have had these things made himself?"

Jane was examining the abacus. She grimaced and drew back. "If he did, I don't like him. But see if you can find out, Denny."

Paradine nodded. "I shall."

He drank his highball, frowning. He was vaguely worried. But he wasn't scared—yet.

Rex Holloway was a fat, shiny man, with a bald head and thick spectacles, above which his thick, black brows lay like bushy caterpillars. Paradine brought him home to dinner one night a week later. Holloway did not appear to watch the children, but nothing they did or said was lost on him. His gray eyes, shrewd and bright, missed little.

The toys fascinated him. In the living room the three adults gathered around the table, where the playthings had been placed. Holloway studied them carefully as he listened to what Jane and Paradine had to say. At last he broke his silence.

"I'm glad I came here tonight. But not completely. This is very disturbing, you know."

"Eh?" Paradine stared, and Jane's face showed her consternation. Holloway's next words did not calm them.

"We are dealing with madness."

He smiled at the shocked looks they gave him. "All children are mad, from an adult viewpoint. Ever read Hughes' 'High Wind in Jamaica'?"

"I've got it." Paradine secured the little book from its shelf. Holloway extended a hand, took it, and flipped the pages till he had found the place he wanted. He read aloud:

"'Babies of course are not human—they are animals, and have a very ancient and ramified culture, as cats have, and fishes, and even snakes; the same in kind as these, but much more complicated and vivid, since babies are, after all, one of the most developed species of the lower vertebrates. In short, babies have minds which work in terms and categories of their own which cannot be translated into the terms and categories of the human mind.'"

Jane tried to take that calmly, but couldn't. "You don't mean that Emma—"

"Could you think like your daughter?" Holloway asked. "Listen: 'One can no more think like a baby than one can think like a bee.'"

Paradine mixed drinks. Over his shoulder he said, "You're theorizing quite a bit, aren't you? As I get it, you're implying that babies have a culture of their own, even a high standard of intelligence."

"Not necessarily. There's no yardstick, you see. All I say is that babies think in other ways than we do. Not necessarily *better*—that's a question of relative values. But with a different manner of extension—" He sought for words, grimacing.

"Fantasy," Paradine said, rather rudely, but annoyed because of Emma. "Babies don't have different senses from ours."

"Who said they did?" Holloway demanded. "They use their minds in a different way, that's all. But it's quite enough!"

"I'm trying to understand," Jane said slowly. "All I can think of is my Mixmaster. It can whip up batter and potatoes, but it can squeeze oranges, too."

"Something like that. The brain's a colloid, a very complicated machine. We don't know much about its potentialities. We don't even know how much it can grasp. But it *is* known that the mind becomes conditioned as the human animal matures. It follows certain familiar theorems, and all thought thereafter is pretty well based on patterns taken for granted. Look at this." Holloway touched the abacus. "Have you experimented with it?"

"A little," Paradine said.

"But not much. Eh?"

"Well—"

"Why not?"

"It's pointless," Paradine complained. "Even a puzzle has to have some logic. But those crazy angles—"

"Your mind has been conditioned to Euclid," Holloway said. "So this—thing—bores us, and seems pointless. But a child knows nothing of Euclid. A different sort of geometry from ours wouldn't impress him as being illogical. He believes what he sees."

"Are you trying to tell me that this gadget's got a fourth-dimensional extension?" Paradine demanded.

"Not visually, anyway," Holloway denied. "All I say is that our minds, conditioned to Euclid, can see nothing in this but an illogical tangle of wires. But a child—especially a baby—might see more. Not at first. It'd be a puzzle, of course. Only a child wouldn't be handicapped by too many preconceived ideas."

"Hardening of the thought-arteries," Jane interjected.

Paradine was not convinced. "Then a baby could work calculus better than Einstein? No, I don't mean that. I can see your point, more or less clearly. Only—"

"Well, look. Let's suppose there are two kinds of geometry—we'll limit it, for the sake of the example. Our kind, Euclidean, and another, which we'll call x. X hasn't much relationship to Euclid. It's based on different theorems. Two and two needn't equal four in it; they could equal y_2, or they might not even *equal*. A baby's mind is not yet conditioned, except by certain questionable factors of heredity and environment. Start the infant on Euclid—"

"Poor kid," Jane said.

Holloway shot her a quick glance. "The basis of Euclid. Alphabet blocks. Math, geometry, algebra—they come much later. We're familiar with that development. On the other hand, start the baby with the basic principles of our x logic."

"Blocks? What kind?"

Holloway looked at the abacus. "It wouldn't make much sense to us. But we've been conditioned to Euclid."

Paradine poured himself a stiff shot of whiskey. "That's pretty awful. You're not limiting to math."

"Right! I'm not limiting it at all. How can I? I'm not conditioned to x logic."

"There's the answer," Jane said, with a sigh of relief. "Who is? It'd take such a person to make the sort of toys you apparently think these are."

Holloway nodded, his eyes, behind the thick lenses, blinking. "Such people may exist."

"Where?"

"They might prefer to keep hidden."

"Supermen?"

"I wish I knew. You see, Paradine, we've got yardstick trouble again. By our standards these people might seem super-doopers in certain respects. In others they might seem moronic. It's not a quantitative difference; it's qualitative. They *think* different. And I'm sure we can do things they can't."

"Maybe they wouldn't want to," Jane said.

Paradine tapped the fused gadgetry on the box. "What about this? It implies—"

"A purpose, sure."

"Transportation?"

"One thinks of that first. If so, the box might have come from anywhere."

"Where—things are—*different?*" Paradine asked slowly.

"Exactly. In space, or even time. I don't know; I'm a pyschologist. Unfortunately I'm conditioned to Euclid, too."

"Funny place it must be," Jane said. "Denny, get rid of those toys."

"I intend to."

Holloway picked up the crystal cube. "Did you question the children much?"

Paradine said, "Yeah. Scott said there were people in that cube when he first looked. I asked him what was in it now."

"What did he say?" The psychologist's eyes widened.

"He said they were building a place. His exact words. I asked him who—people? But he couldn't explain."

"No, I suppose not," Holloway muttered. "It must be progressive. How long have the children had these toys?"

"About three months, I guess."

"Time enough. The perfect toy, you see, is both instructive and mechanical. It should do things, to interest a child, and it should teach, preferably unobtrusively. Simple problems at first. Later—"

"*X* logic," Jane said, white-faced.

Paradine cursed under his breath. "Emma and Scott are perfectly normal!"

"Do you know how their minds work—now?"

Holloway didn't pursue the thought. He fingered the doll. "It would be interesting to know the conditions of the place where these things came from. Induction doesn't help a great deal, though. Too many factors are missing. We can't visualize a world based on the *x* factor—environment adjusted to minds thinking in *x* patterns. This luminous network inside the doll. It could be anything. It could exist inside us, though we haven't discovered it yet. When we find the right stain—" He shrugged. "What do you make of this?"

It was a crimson globe, two inches in diameter, with a protruding knob upon its surface.

"What could anyone make of it?"

"Scott? Emma?"

"I hadn't even seen it till about three weeks ago. Then Emma started to play with it." Paradine nibbled his lip. "After that, Scott got interested."

"Just what do they do?"

"Hold it up in front of them and move it back and forth. No particular pattern of motion."

"No Euclidean pattern," Holloway corrected. "At first they couldn't understand the toy's purpose. They had to be educated up to it."

"That's horrible," Jane said.

"Not to them. Emma is probably quicker at understanding x than is Scott, for her mind isn't yet conditioned to this environment."

Paradine said, "But I can remember plenty of things I did as a child. Even as a baby."

"Well?"

"Was I—mad—then?"

"The things you don't remember are the criterion of your madness," Holloway retorted. "But I use the word 'madness' purely as a convenient symbol for the variation from the known human norm. The arbitrary standard of sanity."

Jane put down her glass. "You've said that induction was difficult, Mr. Holloway. But it seems to me you're making a great deal of it from very little. After all, these toys—"

"I *am* a psychologist, and I've specialized in children. I'm not a layman. These toys mean a great deal to me, chiefly because they mean so little."

"You might be wrong."

"Well, I rather hope I am. I'd like to examine the children."

Jane rose in arms. "How?"

After Holloway had explained, she nodded, though still a bit hesitantly. "Well, that's all right. But they're not guinea pigs."

The psychologist patted the air with a plump hand. "My dear girl! I'm not a Frankenstein. To me the individual is the prime factor—naturally, since I work with minds. If there's anything wrong with the youngsters, I want to cure them."

Paradine put down his cigarette and slowly watched blue smoke spiral up, wavering in an unfelt draft. "Can you give a prognosis?"

"I'll try. That's all I can say. If the undeveloped minds have been turned into the x channel, it's necessary to divert them back. I'm not saying that's the wisest thing to do, but it probably is from our standards. After all, Emma and Scott will have to live in this world."

"Yeah. Yeah. I can't believe there's much wrong. They seem about average, thoroughly normal."

"Superficially they may seem so. They've no reason for acting abnormally, have they? And how can you tell if they—think differently?"

"I'll call 'em," Paradine said.

"Make it informal, then. I don't want them to be on guard."

Jane nodded toward the toys. Holloway said, "Leave the stuff there, eh?"

But the psychologist, after Emma and Scott were summoned, made no immediate move at direct questioning. He managed to draw Scott unobtrusively into the conversation, dropping key words now and then. Nothing so obvious as a word-association test—co-operation is necessary for that.

The most interesting development occurred when Holloway took up the abacus. "Mind showing me how this works?"

Scott hesitated. "Yes, sir. Like this—" He slid a bead deftly through the maze, in a tangled course, so swiftly that no one was quite sure whether or not it ultimately vanished. It might have been merely legerdemain. Then, again—

Holloway tried. Scott watched, wrinkling his nose.

"That right?"

"Uh-huh. It's gotta go *there*—"

"Here? Why?"

"Well, that's the only way to make it work."

But Holloway was conditioned to Euclid. There was no apparent reason why the bead should slide from this particular wire to the other. It looked like a random factor. Also, Holloway suddenly noticed, this wasn't the path the bead had taken previously, when Scott had worked the puzzle. At least, as well as he could tell.

"Will you show me again?"

Scott did, and twice more, on request. Holloway blinked through his glasses. Random, yes. And a variable. Scott moved the bead along a different course each time.

Somehow, none of the adults could tell whether or not the bead vanished. If they had expected to see it disappear, their reactions might have been different.

In the end nothing was solved. Holloway, as he said good night, seemed ill at ease.

"May I come again?"

"I wish you would," Jane told him. "Any time. You still think—"

He nodded. "The children's minds are not reacting normally. They're not dull at all, but I've the most extraordinary impression that they arrive at conclusions in a way we don't understand. As though they used algebra while we used geometry. The same conclusion, but a different method of reaching it."

"What about the toys?" Paradine asked suddenly.

"Keep them out of the way. I'd like to borrow them, if I may—"

That night Paradine slept badly. Holloway's parallel had been ill-chosen. It led to disturbing theories. The x factor—The children were using the equivalent of algebraic reasoning, while adults used geometry.

Fair enough. Only—

Algebra can give you answers that geometry cannot, since there are certain terms and symbols which cannot be expressed geometrically. Suppose x logic showed conclusions inconceivable to an adult mind?

"Damn!" Paradine whispered. Jane stirred beside him.

"Dear? Can't you sleep either?"

"No." He got up and went into the next room. Emma slept peacefully as a cherub, her fat arm curled around Mr. Bear. Through the open doorway Paradine could see Scott's dark head motionless on the pillow.

Jane was beside him. He slipped his arm around her.

"Poor little people," she murmured. "And Holloway called them mad. I think we're the ones who are crazy, Dennis."

"Uh-huh. We've got jitters."

Scott stirred in his sleep. Without awakening, he called what was obviously a question, though it did not seem to be in any particular language. Emma gave a little mewling cry that changed pitch sharply.

She had not wakened. The children lay without stirring.

But Paradine thought, with a sudden sickness in his middle, it was exactly as though Scott had asked Emma something, and she had replied.

Had their minds changed so that even—sleep—was different to them?

He thrust the thought away. "You'll catch cold. Let's get back to bed. Want a drink?"

"I think I do," Jane said, watching Emma. Her hand reached out blindly toward the child; she drew it back. "Come on. We'll wake the kids."

They drank a little brandy together, but said nothing. Jane cried in her sleep, later.

Scott was not awake, but his mind worked in slow, careful building. Thus—

"They'll take the toys away. The fat man . . . listava dangerous maybe. But the Ghoric direction won't show . . . evankrus dun-hasn't-them. Intransdection . . . bright and shiny. Emma. She's more khopranik-high now than . . . I still don't see how to . . . thavarar lixery dist—"

A little of Scott's thoughts could still be understood. But Emma had become conditioned to x much faster.

She was thinking, too.

Not like an adult or a child. Not even like a human. Except, perhaps, a human of a type shockingly unfamiliar to *genus homo*.

Sometimes Scott himself had difficulty in following her thoughts.

If it had not been for Holloway, life might have settled back into an almost normal routine. The toys were no longer active reminders. Emma still enjoyed her dolls and sand pile, with a thoroughly explicable delight. Scott was satisfied with baseball and his chemical set. They did everything other children did, and evinced few, if any, flashes of abnormality. But Holloway seemed to be an alarmist.

He was having the toys tested, with rather idiotic results. He drew endless charts and diagrams, corresponded with mathematicians, engineers, and other psychologists, and went quietly crazy trying to find rhyme or reason in the construction of the gadgets. The box itself, with its cryptic machinery, told nothing. Fusing had melted too much of the stuff into slag. But the toys—

It was the random element that baffled investigation. Even that was a matter of semantics. For Holloway was convinced that it wasn't really random. There just weren't enough known factors. No adult could work the abacus, for example. And Holloway thoughtfully refrained from letting a child play with the thing.

The crystal cube was similarly cryptic. It showed a mad pattern of colors, which sometimes moved. In this it resembled a kaleidoscope. But the shifting of balance and gravity didn't affect it. Again the random factor.

Or, rather, the unknown. The x pattern. Eventually Paradine and Jane slipped back into something like complacence, with a feeling that the children had been cured of their mental quirk, now that the contributing cause had been removed. Certain of the actions of Emma and Scott gave them every reason to quit worrying.

For the kids enjoyed swimming, hiking, movies, games, the normal functional toys of this particular time-sector. It was true that they failed to master certain rather puzzling mechanical devices which involved some calculation. A three-dimensional jigsaw globe Paradine had picked up, for example. But he found that difficult himself.

Once in a while there were lapses. Scott was hiking with his father one Saturday afternoon, and the two had paused at the summit of a hill. Beneath them a rather lovely valley was spread.

"Pretty, isn't it?" Paradine remarked.

Scott examined the scene gravely. "It's all wrong," he said.

"Eh?"

"I dunno."

"What's wrong about it?"

"Gee—" Scott lapsed into puzzled silence. "I dunno."

The children had missed their toys, but not for long. Emma recovered first, though Scott still moped. He held unintelligible conversations with his sister, and studied meaningless scrawls she drew on paper he supplied. It was almost as though he was consulting her, anent difficult problems beyond his grasp.

If Emma understood more, Scott had more real intelligence, and manipulatory skill as well. He built a gadget with his Meccano set, but was dissatisfied. The apparent cause of his dissatisfaction was exactly why Paradine was relieved when he viewed the structure. It was the sort of thing a normal boy would make, vaguely reminiscent of a cubistic ship.

It was a bit too normal to please Scott. He asked Emma more questions, though in private. She thought for a time, and then made more scrawls with an awkwardly clutched pencil.

"Can you read that stuff?" Jane asked her son one morning.

"Not read it, exactly. I can tell what she means. Not all the time, but mostly."

"Is it writing?"

"N-no. It doesn't mean what it *looks* like."

"Symbolism," Paradine suggested over his coffee.

Jane looked at him, her eyes widening. "Denny—"

He winked and shook his head. Later, when they were alone, he said, "Don't let Holloway upset you. I'm not implying that the kids are corresponding in an unknown tongue. If Emma draws a squiggle and says it's a flower, that's an arbitrary rule—Scott remembers that. Next time she draws the same sort of squiggle, or tries to—well!"

"Sure," Jane said doubtfully. "Have you noticed Scott's been doing a lot of reading lately?"

"I noticed. Nothing unusual, though. No Kant or Spinoza."

"He browses, that's all."

"Well, so did I, at his age," Paradine said, and went off to his morning classes. He lunched with Holloway, which was becoming a daily habit, and spoke of Emma's literary endeavors.

"Was I right about symbolism, Rex?"

The psychologist nodded. "Quite right. Our own language is nothing but arbitrary symbolism now. At least in its application. Look here." On his napkin he drew a very narrow ellipse. "What's that?"

"You mean what does it represent?"

"Yes. What does it suggest to you? It could be a crude representation of—what?"

"Plenty of things," Paradine said. "Rim of a glass. A fried egg. A loaf of French bread. A cigar."

Holloway added a little triangle to his drawing, apex joined to one end of the ellipse. He looked up at Paradine.

"A fish," the latter said instantly.

"Our familiar symbol for a fish. Even without fins, eyes or mouth, it's recognizable, because we've been conditioned to identify this particular shape with our mental picture of a fish. The basis of a rebus. A symbol, to us, means a lot more than what we actually see on paper. What's in your mind when you look at this sketch?"

"Why—a fish."

"Keep going. What do you visualize—everything!"

"Scales," Paradine said slowly, looking into space. "Water. Foam. A fish's eye. The fins. The colors."

"So the symbol represents a lot more than just the abstract idea *fish*. Note the connotation's that of a noun, not a verb. It's harder to express actions by symbolism, you know. Anyway—reverse the process. Suppose you want to make a symbol for some concrete noun, say *bird*. Draw it."

Paradine drew two connected arcs, concavities down.

"The lowest common denominator," Holloway nodded. "The natural tendency is to simplify. Especially when a child is seeing something for the first time and has few standards of comparison. He tries to identify the new thing with what's already familiar to him. Ever notice how a child draws the ocean?" He didn't wait for an answer; he went on.

"A series of jagged points. Like the oscillating line on a seismograph. When I first saw the Pacific, I was about three. I remember it pretty clearly. It looked—tilted. A flat plain, slanted at an angle. The waves were regular triangles, apex upward. Now I didn't *see* them stylized that way, but later, remembering, I had to find some familiar standard of comparison. Which is the only way of getting any conception of an entirely new thing. The average child tries to draw these regular triangles, but his co-ordination's poor. He gets a seismograph pattern."

"All of which means. what?"

"A child sees the ocean. He stylizes it. He draws a certain definite pattern, symbolic, to him, of the sea. Emma's scrawls may be symbols, too. I don't mean that the world looks different to her—brighter, perhaps, and sharper, more vivid and with a slackening of perception above her eye level. What I do mean is that her thought-processes are different, that she translates what she sees into abnormal symbols."

"You still believe—"

"Yes, I do. Her mind has been conditioned unusually. It may be that she breaks down what she sees into simple, obvious patterns—and realizes a significance to those patterns that we can't understand. Like the abacus. She saw a pattern in that, though to us it was completely random."

Paradine abruptly decided to taper off these luncheon engagements with Holloway. The man was an alarmist. His theories were growing more fantastic than ever, and he dragged in anything, applicable or not, that would support them.

Rather sardonically he said, "Do you mean Emma's communicating with Scott in an unknown language?"

"In symbols for which she hasn't any words. I'm sure Scott understands a great deal of those—scrawls. To him, an isosceles triangle may represent any factor, though probably a concrete noun. Would a man who knew nothing of algebra understand what H_2O meant? Would he realize that the symbol could evoke a picture of the ocean?"

Paradine didn't answer. Instead, he mentioned to Holloway Scott's curious remark that the landscape, from the hill, had looked all wrong. A moment later, he was inclined to regret his impulse, for the psychologist was off again.

"Scott's thought-patterns are building up to a sum that doesn't equal this world. Perhaps he's subconsciously expecting to see the world where those toys came from."

Paradine stopped listening. Enough was enough. The kids were getting along all right, and the only remaining disturbing factor was Holloway himself. That night, however, Scott evinced an interest, later significant, in eels.

There was nothing apparently harmful in natural history. Paradine explained about eels.

"But where do they lay their eggs? Or do they?"

"That's still a mystery. Their spawning grounds are unknown. Maybe the Sargasso Sea, or the deeps, where the pressure can help them force the young out of their bodies."

"Funny," Scott said, thinking deeply.

"Salmon do the same thing, more or less. They go up rivers to spawn." Paradine went into detail. Scott was fascinated.

"But that's *right*, dad. They're born in the river, and when they learn how to swim, they go down to the sea. And they come back to lay their eggs, huh?"

"Right."

"Only they wouldn't *come* back," Scott pondered. "They'd just send their eggs—"

"It'd take a very long ovipositor," Paradine said, and vouchsafed some well-chosen remarks upon oviparity.

His son wasn't entirely satisfied. Flowers, he contended, sent their seeds long distances.

"They don't guide them. Not many find fertile soil."

"Flowers haven't got brains, though. Dad, why do people live *here?*"

"Glendale?"

"No—*here*. This whole place. It isn't all there is, I bet."

"Do you mean the other planets?"

Scott was hesitant. "This is only—part—of the big place. It's like the river where the salmon go. Why don't people go on down to the ocean when they grow up?"

Paradine realized that Scott was speaking figuratively. He felt a brief chill. The—ocean?

The young of the species are not conditioned to live in the completer world of their parents. Having developed sufficiently, they enter that world. Later they breed. The fertilized eggs are buried in the sand, far up the river, where later they hatch.

And they learn. Instinct alone is fatally slow. Especially in the case of a specialized genus, unable to cope even with this world, unable to feed or drink or survive, unless someone has foresightedly provided for those needs.

The young, fed and tended, would survive. There would be incubators and robots. They would survive, but they would not know how to swim downstream, to the vaster world of the ocean.

So they must be taught. They must be trained and conditioned in many ways.

Painlessly, subtly, unobtrusively. Children love toys that do things— and if those toys teach at the same time—

In the latter half of the nineteenth century an Englishman sat on a grassy bank near a stream. A very small girl lay near him, staring up at the sky. She had discarded a curious toy with which she had been playing, and now was murmuring a wordless little song, to which the man listened with half an ear.

"What was that, my dear?" he asked at last.

"Just something I made up, Uncle Charles."

"Sing it again." He pulled out a notebook.

The girl obeyed.

"Does it mean anything?"

She nodded. "Oh, yes. Like the stories I tell you, you know."

"They're wonderful stories, dear."

"And you'll put them in a book some day?"

"Yes, but I must change them quite a lot, or no one would understand. But I don't think I'll change your little song."

"You mustn't. If you did, it wouldn't mean anything."

"I won't change that stanza, anyway," he promised. "Just what does it mean?"

"It's the way out, I think," the girl said doubtfully. "I'm not sure yet. My magic toys told me."

"I wish I knew what London shop sold those marvelous toys!"

"Mamma bought them for me. She's dead. Papa doesn't care."

She lied. She had found the toys in a box one day, as she played by the Thames. And they were indeed wonderful.

Her little song—Uncle Charles thought it didn't mean anything. (He wasn't her real uncle, she parenthesized. But he was nice.) The song meant a great deal. It was the way. Presently she would do what it said, and then—

But she was already too old. She never found the way.

Paradine had dropped Holloway. Jane had taken a dislike to him, naturally enough, since what she wanted most of all was to have her fears calmed. Since Scott and Emma acted normally now, Jane felt satisfied. It was partly wishful-thinking, to which Paradine could not entirely subscribe.

Scott kept bringing gadgets to Emma for her approval. Usually she'd shake her head. Sometimes she would look doubtful. Very occasionally she would signify agreement. Then there would be an hour of laborious, crazy scribbling on scraps of note paper, and Scott, after studying the notations, would arrange and rearrange his rocks, bits of machinery, candle ends, and assorted junk. Each day the maid cleaned them away, and each day Scott began again.

He condescended to explain a little to his puzzled father, who could see no rhyme or reason in the game.

"But why this pebble right here?"

"It's hard and round, dad. It *belongs* there."

"So is this one hard and round."

"Well, that's got vaseline on it. When you get that far, you can't *see* just a hard round thing."

"What comes next? This candle?"

Scott looked disgusted. "That's toward the end. The iron ring's next."

It was, Paradine thought, like a Scout trail through the woods, markers in a labyrinth. But here again was the random factor. Logic halted—familiar logic—at Scott's motives in arranging the junk as he did.

Paradine went out. Over his shoulder he saw Scott pull a crumpled piece of paper and a pencil from his pocket, and head for Emma, who was squatted in a corner thinking things over.

Well—

Jane was lunching with Uncle Harry, and, on this hot Sunday afternoon there was little to do but read the papers. Paradine settled himself in the coolest place he could find, with a Collins, and lost himself in the comic strips.

An hour later a clatter of feet upstairs roused him from his doze. Scott's voice was crying exultantly, "This is it, Slug! Come on—"

Paradine stood up quickly, frowning. As he went into the hall the telephone began to ring. Jane had promised to call—

His hand was on the receiver when Emma's faint voice squealed with excitement. Paradine grimaced. What the devil was going on upstairs?

Scott shrieked, "Look out! This way!"

Paradine, his mouth working, his nerves ridiculously tense, forgot the phone and raced up the stairs. The door of Scott's room was open.

The children were vanishing.

They went in fragments, like thick smoke in a wind, or like movement in a distorting mirror. Hand in hand they went, in a direction Paradine could not understand, and as he blinked there on the threshold, they were gone.

"Emma!" he said, dry-throated. *"Scotty!"*

On the carpet lay a pattern of markers, pebbles, an iron ring—junk. A random pattern. A crumpled sheet of paper blew toward Paradine. He picked it up automatically.

"Kids. Where are you? Don't hide—

"Emma! SCOTTY!"

Downstairs the telephone stopped its shrill, monotonous ringing. Paradine looked at the paper he held.

It was a leaf torn from a book. There were interlineations and marginal notes, in Emma's meaningless scrawl. A stanza of verse had been so underlined and scribbled over that it was almost illegible, but Paradine was thoroughly familiar with "Through the Looking Glass." His memory gave him the words—

> 'Twas brillig, and the slithy toves
> Did gyre and gimbel in the wabe.
> All mimsy were the borogoves,
> And the mome raths outgrabe.

Idiotically he thought: Humpty Dumpty explained it. A wabe is the plot of grass around a sundial. A sundial. Time—It has something to do with time. A long time ago Scotty asked me what a wabe was. Symbolism. *'Twas brillig—*

A perfect mathematical formula, giving all the conditions, in symbolism the children had finally understood. The junk on the floor. The toves had to be made slithy—vaseline?—and they had to be placed in a certain relationship, so that they'd gyre and gimbel. *Lunacy!*

But it had not been lunacy to Emma and Scott. They thought differently. They used *x* logic. Those notes Emma had made on the page— she'd translated Carroll's words into symbols both she and Scott could understand.

The random factor had made sense to the children. They had fulfilled the conditions of the time-space equation. *And the mome raths outgrabe—*

Paradine made a rather ghastly little sound, deep in his throat. He looked at the crazy pattern on the carpet. If he could follow it, as the kids had done— But he couldn't. The pattern was senseless. The random factor defeated him. He was conditioned to Euclid.

Even if he went insane, he still couldn't do it. It would be the wrong kind of lunacy.

His mind had stopped working now. But in a moment the stasis of incredulous horror would pass— Paradine crumpled the page in his fingers. "Emma, Scotty," he called in a dead voice, as though he could expect no response.

Sunlight slanted through the open windows, brightening the golden pelt of Mr. Bear. Downstairs the ringing of the telephone began again.

* * *

According to the story, what does the learning process consist of? That is, how does a human being go about learning in order to become what we understand as human? And how is language important to this process? What is meant by such terms as *"x* patterns" or *"x* logic"? How about a term like "conditioned to Euclid"? Can you see any justification for Padgett's use of Lewis Carroll in the story? (It is assumed you will know who Lewis Carroll was.)

But the story is built on the possibility that the whole process of this learning as we know and accept it may obscure something. Obscure what?

The story is science fiction, a fantasy. And yet it has been said of fantasy that one of its functions is to make you resee the familiar from a new angle, to recover a freshness of vision the effect of which is to cause you to realize that all you thought "you had (or knew) was dangerous and potent, not really effectively chained [but] free and wild; no more yours than [it was] you" (J. R. R. Tolkien, "On Fairy-Stories"). William J. J. Gordon puts it this way:

> To break through toward a creative act, it is necessary to twist out of phase whatever conventional laws appear to hold. This does not mean that it is necessary to defy all the basic hypotheses of our phenomenology, but that it is necessary to defy them *apparently*. Then, through the cracks which appear when the laws are twisted out of phase (all this attained through conscious self-deceit), things can be seen in a new way. So long as the rules are accepted as immutable "laws of vision" the world always will appear to be the same and no novelties can be discovered or fabricated. Many highly trained people naturally tend to think in terms of the dogma of their own technology and it frightens them to twist their conventions out of phase. Their conventions sometimes constitute a background of knowledge upon which they rely for their emotional stability. Such experts do not want cracks to appear. They identify their psychic order with the cosmic order and any cracks are signs of their orderly cosmos breaking up.
>
> *—William J. J. Gordon *

How does Padgett's story enable you to see the process of education —specifically its benefits and liabilities—in a new way, from a new angle?

* From pp. 96, 127, and 128 in *Synectics,* by William J. J. Gordon. Copyright © 1961 by William J. J. Gordon. By permission of Harper & Row, Publishers, Inc.

26. *Edward Gorey*

Here is a story:

THE WILLOWDALE HANDCAR

BY EDWARD GOREY

OR

THE RETURN OF THE BLACK DOLL

 Afterwards a gold ring embellished with leaves, grapes, etc. was found; inside were engraved IRON HILLS and the letters D.M.G., which last stood for the words 'Don't move, Gertrude'.

One summer afternoon in Willowdale Edna,
Harry, and Sam wandered down to the railroad
station to see if anything was doing.

There was nothing on the platform but some empty
crates. 'Look!' said Harry, pointing to a handcar
on the siding. 'Let's take it and go for a ride.'

Soon they were flying along the tracks at a great
rate. Little Grace Sprocket, playing in a homemade mud puddle, watched them go by with
longing.

At Bogus Corners, the next town down the line,
they stopped to buy soda pop and gingersnaps
at Mr Queevil's store. 'How are things over
in Willowdale?' he asked. 'Dull' they said.

A few minutes after they were on their way again,
they saw a house burning down in a field.
'Whooee!' said Sam. 'The engines will never
be in time to save it.'

The next morning they wrote postcards to everybody, telling them what they were doing and
adding that they didn't know exactly when
they would be back.

At 10:17 the *Turnip Valley Express* rushed past.
A frantic face was pressed against a window
of the parlor car.

'Gracious!' said Edna. 'I believe that was Nellie
Flim. We were chums at Miss Underfoot's Seminary.
I wonder what can have been the matter.'

In Chutney Falls they hunted up the cemetery
and peered at the tombstones of Harry's mother's
family.

Later they ran into Nellie's beau, Dick Hammerclaw,
the local telegraph operator. He asked if they'd
seen her. He seemed upset.

Near Gristleburg they saw a palatial mansion on a
bluff. 'That's O Altitudo,' said Sam,'the home of
Titus W. Blotter, the financier. Come to think of it,
Nellie is his upstairs maid.'

Several days later a touring car drew up alongside
them. The driver called out something unintelligible
concerning Dick before he shot away out of sight.

An undated fragment of the 'Willowdale Triangle'
they found caught in a tie informed them that
Wobbling Rock had finally fallen on a family
having a picnic.

In Dogear Junction they paid a call on Edna's
cousins, the Zeph Claggs. He showed them a few
of the prizes from his collection of over 7,000 glass
telephone-pole insulators.

The following week Mount Smith came into
view in the distance; dark clouds were piling
up behind it.

During the thunderstorm that ensued, a flash
of lightning revealed a figure creeping up
the embankment.

Some months went by, and still they had not returned to Willowdale.

They visited the ruins of the Crampton vinegar works, which had been destroyed by a mysterious explosion the preceding fall.

At Wunksieville they rescued an infant who was
hanging from a hook intended for mailbags.

'How much she resembles Nellie!' said Edna. They
turned her over to the matron of the orphanage
in Stovepipe City.

From the trestle over Peevish Gorge they spied the wreck of a touring car at the bottom. 'I don't see Dick's friend anywhere,' said Harry.

In Violet Springs they learned that Mrs Regera Dowdy was not receiving visitors, but through a window they were able to see the desk on which she wrote her poems.

As they were going along the edge of the Sogmush River, they passed a man in a canoe. 'If I'm not mistaken,' said Edna, 'he was lurking inside the vinegar works'.

Between West Elbow and Penetralia they almost ran over someone who was tied to the track. It proved to be Nellie.

Despite their entreaties, she insisted on being
left at the first grade crossing, where she got
on a bicycle and rode away.

That evening they attended a baked-bean supper
at the Halfbath Methodist Church. 'They're
all right,' said Sam, 'but they're not a patch
on Mrs Umlaut's back home'.

A week later they noticed someone who might have been Nellie walking in the grounds of the Weedhaven Laughing Academy.

On Sunday afternoon they saw Titus W. Blotter in his shirtsleeves plunge into the Great Trackless Swamp.

In Hiccupboro they counted the cannon balls in the pyramids on the courthouse lawn.

At sunset they entered a tunnel in the Iron Hills and did not come out the other end.

How do you interpret *The Willowdale Handcar?* What "happens" in the story, so far as you are concerned? What does the story seem to mean? In addressing these questions express as clearly as you can your understanding of the relationships between the various characters, between the characters and events. What do you do with such details as the Crampton vinegar works, those glass telephone-pole insulators? How about the baked-bean supper at the Halfbath Methodist Church? And the black doll (on Mrs. Regera Dowdy's desk), where does it come in? Are these Symbols? Red Herrings? Is this a story for children? For those who are Children no longer? For someone else?

However you locate yourself with these matters, bear in mind that it is two languages you are dealing with here: Gorey's use of the English language as well as the language of his drawings. Your interpretation ought to reflect how you see these two languages relating to each other. Do Gorey's drawings help you to understand what his words mean? The other way around? Or would you rather express the relation in some other way?

You have made an interpretation of *The Willowdale Handcar.* You have put things together in a certain way, arranged things so that they make sense. You have made a pattern. There is a way in which your whole life may be said to be based on the making of interpretations in very much the same way you made an interpretation of Gorey's story. Yet you do not in your life always have the same difficulty making interpretations that you did with Gorey. Nor is your attitude toward the interpretations you make always the same as your attitude toward the interpretation you have made of *The Willowdale Handcar.* Why not?

What does your experience with *The Willowdale Handcar* enable you to see in a new way, from a new angle, about the process of interpretation—and about what it means to make one?

27. Seeing Other Ways of Seeing

Lewis Padgett and Edward Gorey are not the only writers to have dealt with the implications of what it means to be "conditioned to Euclid." Here is an account of the significance of the invention of a system of non-Euclidean geometry. When you come to class, know more about Lobachevsky than you can gather from the passage, and be able to supply the written source or sources for your information.

One classic example [of speculative play with logical systems] is Lobachevsky's invention of non-Euclidean geometry. . . . The new geometry . . . seemed at first mere wilful play, irresponsible in fact. The closed system of Euclidean geometry was judged to be true, not only logical in itself, but also descriptive of the nature of the space as experienced. This representative accuracy of Euclidean geometry is "true" of everyday spatial relationships in that it enables us to handle those relationships with "reasonable" accuracy. However, this "representative accuracy" is a function of traditional ways of perceiving and categorizing our experience of everyday space, traditional ways which are accepted but are neither true or untrue. Lobachevsky's invention has therefore two important consequences: 1) It questions the degree of "representative accuracy" which was traditionally attributed to the Euclidean system. Thus Lobachevsky's system tended to make the familiar strange. When we live with the familiar system without questioning it, we lose our awareness of the unfounded (even questionable) assumptions which underlie the system and our acceptance of it. We attribute a false concreteness to what in reality is only a symbolic representation, a conceptual tool. When the established system was questioned in a "strange" way by Lobachevsky the system, its assumptions, and its implications became more clear for what it was. 2) Lobachevsky's invention also makes it possible at least to conceive (if not to see) other ways of interpreting the human experience of space. Contemporary concepts of the nature of the nuclear astro-physical world would be impossible if we were still locked into the assumption that Euclidean geometry provides the final symbolic language for the expression of spatial relationships.

Language itself—mathematical symbols or words and phrases —when combined into a logical self-consistent pattern threatens constantly to deceive us as being "concrete," as not only expressing ways of thinking, but also being the way things in themselves are. This threat to constructive imagination assumed two interrelated forms:

1) over-development of expertly elaborated systems of internal consistency; 2) over-development of "apparent" and everyday concreteness. Thus Euclidean geometry, over-developed as a self-consistent system, tends to atrophy in a meaningless closed circle of expertise. Over-developed as concrete and self-evidently valid, it atrophies by becoming confused with a representative description of actual space.

—William J. J. Gordon *

You may never have invented a new geometry. You may never have shaped a fantasy as does Lewis Padgett. You may never have used nonsense as a way of making a joke about the "false concreteness" we attach to symbolic representations of our experience. But you have had the experience of questioning the "representative accuracy" of your way of seeing something, of becoming aware, perhaps all of a sudden, that your way of seeing something was no more than that—the expression of a way of thinking rather than "the way things in themselves are." You have also, as a consequence, been able "to conceive (if not to see) other ways of interpreting" that something.

Choose such a moment from your experience and describe it in detail. Make clear in your description what your original seeing consisted of. Make clear also what it was exactly that made you aware that your way of seeing something was no more than that. Finally, make clear what it meant to see your way of seeing as only a way of seeing. There were those other ways of seeing that you had become aware of: Were they a comfort? A horror? Of no consequence? Where were you left with your experience in this instance? What were you left with?

* W. J. J. Gordon, *Synectics, op. cit.,* pp. 125–126.

28. The Man from Mars

Here is an opportunity for you to do some teaching. Assume that you are explaining life on this world to a Stranger from Mars. He says to you something like this:

"On New Year's Day in the Rose Bowl Northwestern University beat the University of California 20–14 before an estimated crowd of 92,000. On the next day, Sunday, the New York *Times* reported that one of the touchdowns was made as follows: 'Murakowski carried the ball to the California one-yard line and on the next play took it across.' On Monday the *Times* published a photograph of a goal line fumble that had been recovered by California. The officials had ruled that Murakowski had the ball in his possession when he crossed the goal line. In the photograph the ball is in the air and Murakowski is a yard short of the goal line. Murakowski said when shown the photograph, 'I'm sure I was across. . . . Somebody tackled me from behind and pulled me back. That's when I fumbled.'

"The same photograph shows the California tackler with his right arm stretched out, his palm held stiffly back, as if he had just driven the ball from Murakowski's arms. The ball is in the air and falling.

"Another photograph of the same play shows Northwestern Halfback Tom Worthington apparently using an illegal double stiff-arm or shove in blocking Bob Celeri, California corner back. Worthington said that he had used a high shoulder and arms block on Celeri and added that the photo must have been snapped as he was 'following through and starting to fall.'

"The newspaper reports that when the Northwestern coach boarded the Ambassador flight he said, 'It was a wonderful trip.'

"When I put all these items together," says the Martian, "they do not make sense to me. Where I come from our people are interested only in what really happens and we have no trouble learning what really happens either. In your world no one seems to know what really happened in this game."

Your problem here is to straighten out this Martian, to teach him about life in your world. In formulating a way to address him, you may care to take into consideration that the Martian is carrying a device that looks very much like a ray gun and seems in no mood for evasiveness. He expects answers that are straight and complete. Remember, this Martian is armed and dangerous. Without directness, you will be shot down. Without some ability to elaborate, you will be shot down.

Begin by making a list of items, as the Martian calls them (and what do you call them?), in this narrative, and explain how and why they do not go together, what it is the Martian means by saying that "no one seems to know what really happened in this game."

In one sense, of course, no one does know what really happened in this game. Concede this to the Martian by explaining as fully (and as graciously) as possible just how it is so.

But in another sense, we, the inhabitants of this universe, do know what happened in this game. Explain to the Martian how this is so.

You had better assume that the Martian is telling the truth when he says that his people are interested only in what really happens and that they have no trouble learning what really happens. Though you might not want to offer your conclusions to the Martian, what can you infer from his statement about what life on Mars must be like? What must learning consist of there?

But even if we assume the existence of a Man from Mars, this whole exercise is based on an impossibility, a contradiction, is it not? The Man from Mars cannot have come from the kind of world he says he does and have spoken to you so as to make you understand him. Nor could you explain anything to such a creature. Why not?

29. The Risk of Education

Eve—who was under the influence of a seducer, not a teacher—is perhaps the last person to have blamelessly pretended that education is a riskless experience. If a little learning is a dangerous thing, there is still some question as to whether a lot of learning is the opposite of dangerous, for a learner cannot always predict the consequences of his learning. A student cannot always foresee all of the implications of what it means to become a student. Here, for example, is a dramatization of what can happen to someone who decides to become a learner:

From the winter of 1821, when I first read Bentham, and especially from the commencement of the *Westminster Review,* I had what might truly be called an object in life; to be a reformer of the world. My conception of my own happiness was entirely identified with this object. The personal sympathies I wished for were those of fellow labourers in this enterprise. I endeavoured to pick up as many flowers as I could by the way; but as a serious and permanent personal satisfaction to rest upon, my whole reliance was placed on this; and I was accustomed to felicitate myself on the certainty of a happy life which I enjoyed, through placing my happiness in something durable and distant, in which some progress might be always making, while it could never be exhausted by complete attainment. This did very well for several years, during which the general improvement going on in the world and the idea of myself as engaged with others in struggling to promote it, seemed enough to fill up an interesting and animated existence. But the time came when I awakened from this as from a dream. It was in the autumn of 1826. I was in a dull state of nerves, such as everybody is occasionally liable to; unsusceptible to enjoyment or pleasurable excitement; one of those moods when what is pleasure at other times, becomes insipid or indifferent; the state, I should think, in which converts to Methodism usually are, when smitten by their first "conviction of sin." In this frame of mind it occurred to me to put the question directly to myself: "Suppose that all your objects in life were realized; that all the changes in institutions and opinions which you are looking forward to, would be completely effected at this very instant: would this be a great joy and happiness to you?" And an irrepressible self-consciousness distinctly answered, "No!" At this my heart sank within me: the whole foundation on which my life was constructed fell down. All my happiness was to have been found in the continual pursuit of this end. The end had ceased to charm, and how could there ever again be any interest in the means? I seemed to have nothing left to live for. . . . In vain I sought relief from my favourite books; those memorials of past nobleness and greatness from which I had always hitherto drawn strength and animation. I read them now without feeling, or with the accustomed feeling *minus* all its charms; and I became persuaded, that my love of mankind, and of excellence for its own sake, had worn itself out. . . . I frequently asked myself, if I could, or if I was bound to go on living, when life must be passed in this manner. I generally answered to myself, that I did not think I could possibly bear it beyond a year. When, however, not more than half that duration of time had elapsed, a small ray of light broke in upon my gloom. I was reading, accidentally, Marmontel's "Memoires," and came to the passage which relates his father's death, the distressed position of the family, and the sudden inspiration by which he, then a mere boy, felt and made them feel that he would be everything to them—would supply the place of all that they had lost. A vivid conception of the scene and its feelings came over me, and I was moved to tears. From this moment my burden grew lighter. The oppression of the thought that all feeling was dead within me, was gone. I was no longer hopeless: I was not a stock or a stone. I had still, it seemed, some of the material out of which all worth of character, and all capacity for happiness, are made.

—John Stuart Mill *

Mill, as you can see, is what could be called a good student, a good learner. Yet had he not created from the language systems of Bentham and the *Westminster Review* a language of his own with which to see the world, would he have had to experience the depression that he did? If he had not got into the pernicious habit of putting questions to himself, would he have had any trouble? It is true that Mill seems to have made something of a recovery, but that was just an accident, wasn't it? Mill was just lucky?

*   *   *

Where do you find yourself with what could be called the risk of education?

Though we all believe that it is a good thing to change one's mind, though in our ordinary talk about education the open mind is praised, the closed mind condemned, there are parts of the present, and future, about which we are already decided, about which, like Mill, none of us intend to change if we can help it. What sort of person would believe that you should change your mind all the time about everything indefinitely?

* *The Autobiography of John Stuart Mill,* "A Crisis in My Mental History," 1873.

But to judge from Mill's experience, it is sometimes difficult to help it. It is difficult to know the limits of an idea.

Write a paper in which you state a belief that you do not intend to change your mind about. Since this is a belief you will be talking about, no one can argue with you about it with propriety (this does not mean that no one can comment on the sentence or paragraph structure of what you write). State your belief and then deal with the following questions.

What safeguards are you taking to protect this belief? Are there certain discussions you just turn away from? Is there evidence you simply refuse to consider? What exactly are your defenses? How do you use them?

But no matter how intricate your defenses, they may not be adequate, not if you intend to become a student. Using your particular belief as an example, explain just why this is so.

It is, of course, possible for someone to associate himself with an educational institution, with the educational process, without attempting to become a student. Yet many do make this attempt, many people who believe in what they believe in just as strongly as you believe in what you believe in. What do you imagine would make the risk of education worth running for such people? Or is it that they are ignorant of the fact that they are running a risk? All of them? All of us?

Speaking just for yourself, knowing what you know, do you think it worth it for you to attempt to become a student?

30. Putting Things Together

From cradle to grave this problem of running order through chaos, direction through space, discipline through freedom, unity through multiplicity, has always been and must always be, the task of education. . . . At the utmost, the active-minded young man should ask of his teacher only mastery of his tools. The young man himself, the subject of education, is a certain form of energy; the object to be gained is economy of his force; the training is partly the clearing away of obstacles, partly the direct application of effort. Once acquired, the tools and models may be thrown away.°

* * *

This is the last paper you will write for this course. It is an opportunity for you to put some things together for yourself, whatever it is you care to connect in whatever order you choose.

Imagine someone who has just read over everything you have read for this course this term saying something like this to you:

"What does it mean exactly that the real subject of this course is language, but that the metaphor used to talk about it is teaching and learning? What does teaching and learning have to do with language? *Your* learning specifically? And what does this have to do with your writing? Are you supposed to have become a writer or what?"

Write a paper in which you attempt to answer him.

You might begin by rereading the materials of the course yourself. You may also wish to recall conversations you have had about the course or in it. Most important, you will want to read back over your own work, for it is not *a* course you are going to be talking about in this paper, but *your* course. It is not the experience of a *we* (either supposed or actual) that this someone is interested in, but *your* experience, the experience of an *I,* of another someone. For this reason you might therefore wish to consider whether you are sure that you want to say obvious things such as "My writing has improved" (or "failed to improve"). Do you really want to bother with trying to guess what you think someone else wants you to say? Do you really want to bother at this point with the clichés? But how are you going to say that you're better than, or worse than, or just the same as you were without simply asking someone to take your word for it?

° *The Education of Henry Adams,* 1906.

Suppose you aren't the writer that you want to be? Does this mean that your time has been wasted? That you wasted your time? Any other possibilities?

Perhaps it would be possible to handle these matters in terms of a situation, in terms of a specific instance of teaching or learning where people did things, moved and talked?

A good place to begin thinking out a way to address the problem of this paper might be to consider specifically the first paper you wrote for the course which has just been returned to you. Who were you in that paper? Who are you now? Have you changed your mind about anything? What is there you haven't changed your mind about?